Organization and Staffing of the Libraries of Columbia University

Organization and Staffing of the Libraries of Columbia University

A Case Study

Prepared by Booz, Allen & Hamilton, Inc.

Sponsored by the **ASSOCIATION OF RESEARCH LIBRARIES**
in cooperation with the American Council on Education,
under a grant from the Council
on Library Resources

REDGRAVE INFORMATION RESOURCES CORP.
Westport, Connecticut

Copyright © 1973 by the Association of Research Libraries

Library of Congress Catalog Card Number: 72–13447
First published in 1973

Library of Congress Cataloging in Publication Data

Booz, Allen and Hamilton, inc.
  Organization and staffing of the libraries of
Columbia University.

  "Sponsored by the Association of Research
Libraries in cooperation with the American
Council on Education."
    1. Columbia University. Libraries.
2. Libraries, University and college--Administration
--Case studies.   3.   Research libraries--
Administration--Case studies.   I.   Association of
Research Libraries.   II.   American Council on
Education.   III.   Title.
Z733.N664B6   1973   027.7'747'1   72–13447
ISBN 0–88276–002–5

Redgrave Information Resources Corp.
53 Wilton Road, Westport, Connecticut 06880

Printed in the United States of America
Designed by Laurel Brown

Contents

Contents

Contents

Index of
Exhibits

Foreword

The Association of Research Libraries has long had an interest in improving the administration of university libraries. The Association has given evidence of this interest in various ways. Since 1944 it has compiled and published the annual statistics of its members. Several of its committees (for example, the Committee on Automation, the ARL-ACRL Joint Committee on University Library Standards, and the Committee on Training for Research Librarianship) have concerned themselves with specific aspects of library management. Program meetings through the years have emphasized such diverse topics as staff participation in management, minority opportunities in research libraries, and program planning for university libraries.

In recent years the Association's interest in management has become more sharply focused. Largely through the efforts of Warren J. Haas, formerly Director of Libraries at the University of Pennsylvania and currently Vice-President for Information Services and University Librarian at Columbia University, acting on the suggestion of Dr. Fred C. Cole, President of the Council on Library Resources, the Association has taken a series of steps that have brought it to a position of leadership in research in library management. In 1969, the ARL Board of Directors created the Committee on University Library Management with Mr. Haas as Chairman. Next, with the encouragement and support of the Council on Library

Resources, the ARL joined with the American Council on Education to sponsor a comprehensive study of university library management with the consulting firm of Booz, Allen & Hamilton acting as principal investigator. The resulting publication, *Problems in University Management*, has been the point of departure for much subsequent research. In 1970, again with the support of CLR, the Association established the office of University Library Management Studies, and in October of that year Duane E. Webster became Director of that office.

Permanent staff for the Management Office, in particular a full-time professional director, has brought added impetus to the search for solutions to the management problems of university libraries. Working with the Executive Director and staff of the ARL, with the newly formed ARL Commission on the Management of Research Libraries, and with the ARL-ACE Joint Committee on University Library Management, the Management Office has succeeded in making management one of the principal concerns of the membership of the Association. In both the scope and the pace of its undertakings, the Management Office has given impressive evidence of its commitment to the important tasks before it, and it has demonstrated that results can be achieved if qualified personnel and adequate financial support can be brought together.

One of the first tasks of the Office of University Library Management Studies was to join with Booz, Allen & Hamilton in a detailed investigation of the organization and staffing of the libraries of Columbia University. The study was carried out during 1970-71; a summary was published by the Association of Research Libraries in 1972; and periodic progress reports were made to the membership at the Midwinter and Spring meetings of the Association. Now, with the publication of the full report, a wealth of additional detail becomes available for the first time.

The Columbia case study is a direct outgrowth of the earlier ARL-ACE study of problems in university library management. Once again Booz, Allen & Hamilton received advice and counsel from a joint committee made up of representatives of the ARL, the ACE and CLR. In addition, the study team had access throughout the course of the project to a senior staff advisory committee at the Columbia University Libraries.

What were the expectations of the study team in undertaking the Columbia investigation, and how well were those expectations reflected in the findings of the report? Booz, Allen & Hamilton prepared the following outline:

1. To project the future requirements of the Columbia University Libraries.
2. To evaluate the existing organization and staffing of the Columbia University Libraries.
3. To suggest desirable principles of organization and executive staffing.
4. To recommend a plan of library organization.
5. To prescribe a detailed staffing pattern for the Columbia University Libraries.

It finally became clear that the overriding purpose of the study was twofold: to strengthen library services at Columbia University and to provide guidance for the improvement of other university libraries.

The final report of the case study delivers everything promised in the outline and a good deal more. It offers a context for the study. It describes current trends in higher education and their implications for libraries. It provides a full description of the libraries of Columbia University as they presently exist. It suggests changes in organization and staffing to meet new requirements as perceived by the study team. It recommends new management styles and new approaches in the use of professional personnel. Finally, it makes detailed suggestions for implementing the many recommendations of the report calling for change and innovation.

There are many provocative suggestions in this report—some of the more noteworthy ones include:

- a new role for the academic library director
- departures from the traditional departmental structure of libraries
- alternatives to the technical services-readers services division in academic libraries
- closer coordination of all library and information programs on the university campus

- the provision of new staff specialties in order to add new capabilities to library programs
- the enhancement of opportunities for staff involvement in decision-making and policy formulation
- the creation of new career patterns allowing for individual pursuit of professional, scholarly or administrative interests
- the development of organizational capacity for expanded library and information services emphasizing classroom instruction and assistance.

Over and above these specific findings of the Columbia case study are a number of suggestions for implementing the numerous recommendations of the report. Perhaps the most important of these is that the Libraries should establish a Planning Office under the direction of an Assistant University Librarian. This proposal won prompt acceptance and the Planning Office was established in July of 1972. The existence of the Planning Office has contributed significantly to the process of implementing other recommendations of the report.

The effects of the case study, both at Columbia and elsewhere, still lie largely in the future, but already some important results can be cited. The value of the ARL Office of Management Studies has been established, with the result that the Council on Library Resources has awarded the Office a new three year grant to continue its work. With its immediate future assured, the Office is already building upon the foundation provided by the Columbia case study and the earlier Booz, Allen & Hamilton report. It has developed the Management Review and Analysis Program, which is a detailed management self-study technique. The Office has tested this program and revised it and is currently assisting a number of libraries in its application.

This is but one example of how the lessons of the Columbia study may be brought to bear upon the problems of other research libraries. Additional benefits are sure to follow and indeed the Office of Management Studies has formulated plans which will insure a wide sharing of the fruits of this research. There is, however, no real substitute for a careful reading of the report itself. When those who manage research libraries study this report and when they come to understand the number, variety, and significance of its findings, they are sure to gain new insights into how research libraries function. This awareness can, in turn, show us how libraries can better serve those who use them.

Improved library management in the service of the library user—that is precisely what this report is all about.

John P. McDonald
March, 1973

Mr. McDonald, Director of Libraries at the University of Connecicut, was president of ARL in 1972–1973.

MEMBERS OF THE
JOINT ADVISORY COMMITTEE

Mr. Warren J. Haas, Chairman; President (1969–1970), Association of Research Libraries; Director of Libraries, Columbia University

Dr. Willard Boyd, President, University of Iowa

Mr. Douglas W. Bryant, University Librarian, Harvard University

Dr. Allan Cartter, Chancellor, New York University

Dr. Herman H. Fussler, Director of Libraries[1], University of Chicago

Dr. Howard Johnson, President[1], Massachusetts Institute of Technology

Dr. Richard Lyman, President, Stanford University

Mr. John P. McDonald, Director of Libraries, University of Connecticut

Mr. Robert Vosper, University Librarian, University of California at Los Angeles

Dr. Stephen McCarthy[2], Executive Director, Association of Research Libraries

Mr. Louis Martin[2], Associate Executive Director, Association of Research Libraries

Dr. Fred C. Cole[2], President, Council on Library Resources

Mr. Foster Mohrhardt[2], Senior Program Officer, Council on Library Resources

MEMBERS OF THE
SENIOR STAFF ADVISORY COMMITTEE

Mr. Warren J. Haas, Chairman, Director of Libraries

Mr. Donald C. Anthony, Associate Director of Libraries

Mr. Erle P. Kemp, Associate Director for Technical Services

1. Positions held until July, 1971.
2. Ex-officio members.

Mr. Frederick Duda, Assistant Director for Administrative Services
Mr. George Lowy, Librarian, International Affairs Division
Mr. Adolf Placzek, Librarian, Art and Architecture Division

MEMBERS OF THE CONSULTING TEAM

Dr. H. Lawrence Wilsey, Senior Vice President and Managing Officer of the Institutional Group, Booz, Allen & Hamilton Inc.

Mr. Douglas F. Beaven, Associate, Educational and Institutional Division, Booz, Allen & Hamilton Inc.

Dr. Earl C. Bolton, Vice President, Educational and Institutional Division, Booz, Allen & Hamilton Inc.

Mr. Douglas W. Metz, Vice President, Educational and Institutional Division, Booz, Allen & Hamilton Inc.

Mr. Duane E. Webster, Director, Office of University Library Management Studies, Association of Research Libraries

Organization and Staffing of the Libraries of Columbia University

Introduction

The American university is changing today at a more rapid rate than at any time in its history. With new fields of study emerging, academic research and study increasingly cross traditional disciplinary lines and are problem oriented. Colleges and universities are modifying curricula to permit more individualized study. This results in new pressures and opportunities for faculty and students alike. At the same time, in one form or another, collective bargaining by faculty and students as well as by paid staff has affected the governing structures, staffing patterns, and budgets at many institutions across the country. In the 1970s, such changes will continue, perhaps at an even greater pace than ever before.

These developments in higher education have had, and will continue to have, a major impact on the university library—the primary access channel to man's recorded knowledge.

DEVELOPMENTS IN HIGHER EDUCATION

Society's requirements and expectations of universities are increasing and undergoing qualitative changes. The university is being challenged to involve itself more directly in the needs of society while at the same time it is expected to maintain its intellectual and academic integrity. Demands are being made for broader constitutent participation in university decision making by faculty, students and other groups. Increasingly, requirements and demands are being presented forcefully to the university by means of mobilization of group strength.

The objectives as well as the programs of universities are being revised in emphasis and approach to relate more closely and directly to the needs of society. Additional emphasis is being placed on instruction and on the individual initiative of the student rather than on institutional prescription as in the past. In some respects, instruction and research tend to merge as the basic techniques of research become more essential to fulfilling the ends of instruction. Research is being given somewhat less emphasis than in recent decades except in areas, such as urban affairs, that are being accorded high priority by society. Programs of instruction are being revised to serve different mixes of individuals and to make use of new instructional approaches and materials.

University organization and staffing plans are also undergoing rapid and continuing change. Authorities and responsibilities among the governing board, faculty, students, and administration are being redistributed. Top managements are being restructured, and innovative approaches—such as the use of executive teams and presidential cabinets—are being used with growing frequency. Staff assistance, particularly in administrative areas, is being sought by top executives to increase the efficiency and effectiveness of their institutions. Patterns of staffing are being changed. Many universities are seeking ways to increase faculty productivity and new, specialized professional and technical positions are being established. Staff turnover continues to be high in nearly all fields and at all levels.

At the same time that their requirements are increasing and changing, American universities are confronted with growing financial crises. Costs of operation and capital development are increasing more rapidly than income from public and private sources, and there are real limitations on the ability of institutions to meet growing deficits by increasing tuition and fee charges to students. In many institutions of higher education, library costs are among those that are increasing most rapidly.

IMPLICATIONS FOR RESEARCH LIBRARIES

These and other present and impending developments in higher education have major implications for university libraries. Corollary changes will have to be made in the objectives of research libraries as well as in their collections, services, organization and staffing, financial planning and control, and their relationships with other institutions. Specifically, these trends in higher education imply that the organization and staffing of university libraries will need to assure that:

- Plans for university development include well-thought-out plans for libraries and that key library staff are integral participants in the university planning process
- Libraries contribute substantively to planning for the university's changing role in instruction, research, and community service
- Library capabilities needed to support new types of academic programs and to complement new approaches to instruction and research can be developed
- Libraries are organized internally to work effectively with administration, faculty, and other components of the university at the highest levels
- Meaningful priorities can be established to maximize cost effectiveness in collection development, facility utilization, and deployment of needed services and staff
- Staffing patterns allow full use of the highest skills of staff members and enhance their professionalism under effective leadership and supervision
- Libraries, perhaps to a greater extent than any other component of the university, are organized and staffed to plan and implement schemes of interinstitutional and regional cooperation.

Selected major trends in American higher education and their implications for library organization and staffing are outlined in more detail in Appendix A of this report.

In 1969–1970, the Association of Research Libraries, in cooperation with the American Council on Education and the Council on Library Resources, completed a study on problems in university library management. In considering future educational requirements, this investigation found that organizational arrangements in research libraries "are too informal, poorly matched to current and emerging requirements and designed without benefit of modern management approaches" and that these institutions often have "inadequate staffing and provision for staff development."

Following completion of the preliminary investigation, the Association of Research Libraries, again in cooperation with the American Council on Education and the Council on Library Resources, decided that first attention should be given to strengthening the organization and staffing of research libraries. They agreed that, as an initial effort, a case study should be made at a leading university library. Columbia University was selected as the case institution.

In many respects, Columbia University is an exemplary institution for a case study. The leadership of the university, the libraries, and the faculty is dedicated to constructive change and improvement. It can be anticipated that the results of this study will achieve real benefits for the university in the years ahead.

The primary goal of the case study is to help Columbia University prepare for its distinctive future rather than to attempt to produce a prototypical guide for all university libraries. Thus, while the report notes some conclusions of potential significance to many universities and research libraries, it concentrates on the Columbia situation. A separate report to the Association of Research Libraries identifies further study efforts that should be undertaken by the Office of University Library Management Studies from which broader generalizations can be drawn. The hope remains, however, that other institutions will find the Columbia case study interesting and, perhaps, of assistance in matching the organization and staffing plans to their own objectives and needs.

SUMMARY OF RECOMMENDATIONS

Detailed organization and staffing recommendations are presented
in the following chapters of this report, which should be read in
its entirety to comprehend fully what is being proposed. Exhibit
1 summarizes the recommendations in terms of the requirements
that Columbia's libraries will need to meet in the future.

EXHIBIT 1

Columbia University
SUMMARY OF RECOMMENDATIONS THAT WILL HELP
PREPARE THE LIBRARIES OF COLUMBIA UNIVERSITY
FOR THE FUTURE

Action Recommended To Prepare Columbia's Libraries To Meet Future Requirements	Benefits Sought by the Recommendation
A NEW OVERALL PLAN OF ORGANIZATION FOR LIBRARIES SHOULD BE ADOPTED BY COLUMBIA UNIVERSITY TO PREPARE THE LIBRARIES TO PARTICIPATE IN PLANNING AND MEET THE NEEDS OF THE FUTURE	Strengthens Columbia's ability to (1) develop and utilize libraries' resources to (2) meet the wide variety of user requirements ranging from relatively routine first line access to advanced in-depth reference and instructional services.
The University Libraries Should Continue To Be Organized on a Centralized Basis	Continues Columbia's present capacity to plan, develop, and implement the university's information resources on a system-wide basis.
Columbia's Libraries Should Be Headed by a Single Executive Officer With the Title and Status of Vice President and University Librarian	Preserves the present unity of professional leadership and enhances the stature of the university librarian as a top official of the university administration.
He should be a member of the President's cabinet and other top councils of the university.	Places the university librarian in a position to have an impact on university decision making which can have significant far-reaching implications for the library's development.
He should be aided by an Assistant University Librarian for Planning	Provides a critical planning support to assist the university librarian in fulfilling his role and responsibilities.
Working Relationships Should Be Strengthened and Clarified Between the University Libraries and the University's Top Administration and Faculties.	Provides a rationale for formalizing liaison with academic units for purposes of better planning and service evaluation.
A Resources Group should be established to work with the faculty in collection development and preservation by providing in-depth reference service, participating in planning institutional programs, and participating in planning research projects.	Provides a subject-oriented professional library resource that can be drawn upon by faculties where knowledgeable and specialized service is required.
A Formal Approach to Library Planning Should Be Adopted	Strengthens the library's ability to anticipate needs and to govern the use of its limited resources according to established priorities.
The library planning process should be carefully interrelated with university plans.	Recognizes formally the need to both participate in university planning and to develop library resources in the context of the university plans adopted.

EXHIBIT 1

Action Recommended To Prepare Columbia's Libraries To Meet Future Requirements	Benefits Sought by the Recommendation
The Resources Group should comprise professional staff members with outstanding qualifications. Many should be qualified both in the library and scholarly fields.	Frees librarian and other professional staff resources from many routine administrative matters to concentrate their efforts where heavy professional input is required.
The Overall Plan of Organization Should Be Supported by Committees and Advisory Groups	Multiplies the application of staff, faculty, student, and outside expertise to the solution of library problems, and enhances the effectiveness of leadership.
These should provide staff members with opportunities to participate in and contribute to the work of the libraries and the the university.	Strengthens and gives substance to the involvement of staff in library planning and decision making.
A formal approach to planning should be adopted that ensures meaningful involvement of staff.	Provides for systematic ongoing approach to planning.
COLUMBIA'S LIBRARIES SHOULD BE ORGANIZED INTERNALLY IN FIVE MAJOR UNITS MATCHED TO PROGRAM REQUIREMENTS	Enhances functional clarity and professional focus in the plan of organization to better deploy library resources on behalf of the varying needs of the user.
The heads of the units should work together on a professional partnership basis as a top management team.	Assures effective communication and joint planning among the libraries' top management people.
Comprehensive planning is a top management function to which the Vice President and University Librarian should give continuing personal attention and leadership.	Gives top level executive attention to the critical need for effective planning to optimize the use of limited resources where they are most required.
A Resources Group Should Be Established To Be Responsible for Collection Development and Preservation and Other Major Professional Activities Geared to Meeting Advanced User Requirements in Particular	Develops professional staff capabilities that are subject oriented and can be deployed where and when heavily professional service is needed.
The Group should include a Resource Development and Utilization Division for: - Collection development - Backup reference support - Subject oriented faculty and research liaison	Provides organizational cohesion for applying specialized skills on fundamental professional concerns.
A Bibliographic Control Division should be established to exercise administrative control over cataloging activities in all areas of the library system.	Provides for centralized planning and coordination of cataloging activities and the implementation of pertinent policies.

EXHIBIT 1

Action Recommended To Prepare Columbia's Libraries To Meet Future Requirements	Benefits Sought by the Recommendation
A Coordinator of Instructional Programs should be appointed.	Gives system-wide staff leadership to the development of effective instructional programs to serve the academic community.
A Coordinator of Current Awareness Programs should be appointed.	Provides system-wide staff leadership to developing and coordinating the libraries' current awareness activities.
A Services Group Should Be Established To Be Responsible for Providing First-Line Library Services to the Academic Community on a Day-to-Day Basis	Focuses organizational responsibilities and capabilities on the critical need for effective management and administration of basic service delivery and associated support systems in the various library facilities.
Three subject centers should be established including a: - Humanistic and Historical Studies Center - Social Science Center - Science Information Center	Differentiates responsibilities for planning for and providing appropriate access services to meet the distinctive needs of users in three broad subject areas, while assuring overall leadership and coordination under the direction of an Associate University Librarian for Services
Each subject center should be organized internally to include: - Access Services Department - Instructional Materials and Services Department - Allied Libraries	Furthers the development of specialized staff capabilities to assist users in (1) locating and obtaining library materials, (2) in learning how to use library resources effectively, and (3) providing some decentralized units to assure easy access.
A Support Group Should Be Established To Provide Essential Business, Analysis, and Record Production Services	Brings together an array of technical, highly specialized support skills into a tightly organized environment aimed at providing highly efficient services.
The Group should be organized internally to include: - Records and Materials Processing Department - Business Services Department	Provides for grouping of similar and/or interdependent activities administratively for coordinated development and to monitor performance more effectively.
Distinctive Collections, Law and Medical Science Information Libraries Should Report Directly to the Vice President and University Librarian	Continues to regard these specialized units as integral parts of the university's library system, while recognizing their unique user requirements.

EXHIBIT 1

Action Recommended To Prepare Columbia's Libraries To Meet Future Requirements	Benefits Sought by the Recommendations
Highest Level Support and Attention Should Be Given to the Personnel Function	Strengthens library capabilities for forecasting manpower needs and for furthering staff development and growth through ongoing personnel planning and effective training programs.
A Planning Office Should Be Established for Effective Program Planning and Budgeting	Gives recognition and staff support to planning and budgeting as critical for sound top management decision making.
A New Comprehensive Plan of Staffing Should Be Adopted to Include Executive, Librarian, Specialist and Clerical positions	Classifies positions in accordance with the work to be done and the skills required to do the work, enhances career opportunities, emphasizes performance, and heightens job fulfillment.
The plan for structuring positions should be matched to work requirements.	Provides greater clarity in position descriptions and groups positions to more closely match job and skill requirements.
Librarian positions should be redefined to consolidate meaningful professional tasks.	Establishes professional positions that involve exclusively or primarily professional pursuits.
A number of new specialist positions should be established, including priorities such as information specialist, circulation specialist, and reading room attendant.	Groups positions that require specialized competencies but not necessarily those of a trained librarian.
A plan for assigning positions to organization units should be adopted.	Suggests the distribution of positions within the proposed plan of organization according to estimated services to be performed.
Utilize Group Problem Solving Methods to Involve Appropriate Staff in Library Plan- and Development	Ensures that the different skills and resources needed to solve problems and improve performance can be mobilized effectively.
Multiple Reporting Relationships Should Be Adopted for Staff With Service and Resource Responsibilities	Provides greater staffing flexibility to apply critical professional skills efficiently where and as they are needed.
Performance Goals Should Be Established as a Basis for Effective Planning and Evaluation	Improves library capabilities to monitor achievements and evaluate alternatives in terms, for example, of cost effectiveness measures.
Clear Policies Should Be Established and Up-dated Regularly	Provides staff with framework for decision making and taking action, and for guiding implementation of plans.
Program Budgeting Approaches Should Be Developed	Enhances effective decision making by associating costs with proposed program plans so that meaningful priorities can be established within the limited resources available.

EXHIBIT 1

Action Recommended To Prepare Columbia's Libraries To Meet Future Requirements	Benefits Sought by the Recommendation
Approaches to Leadership and Supervision Should Be Oriented to Achievement of Objectives and High Performance	Focuses the efforts of leadership on dynamic problems of improving service rather than just being concerned with control and accountability.
Formal and Informal Means for Improving Working Relationships and Communication Should Be Adopted	Improves coordination between interdependent units and heightens staff awareness and understanding.
Systematic Programs for Staff Growth and Development Should Be Designed	Provides an ongoing process for helping individual staff members to grow professionally and to further their career objectives, as well as fostering an attitude concerned with improving performance.
A Detailed and Comprehensive Plan of Action Should Be Adopted to Guide Implementation	Provides a logical plan for implementing recommendations in an orderly sequence, and for monitoring results.

CHAPTER ONE

The Libraries of Columbia University

Since its origin in 1763 and throughout its history, Columbia University in the City of New York has been noted for its academic programs, faculty, students, and library resources. Today it is one of the nation's leading comprehensive urban universities. During the past decade Columbia, like other institutions of higher learning around the world, has been undergoing and initiating changes in its objectives, programs, and role in society. Columbia, again like most other universities, is in a period of financial crisis.

The challenges and opportunities that lie ahead for Columbia are momentous. The university's Board of Trustees, President, top administration, and faculty are planning for change and are taking daily action to bring about needed change. In the libraries of Columbia University, as in other components of the institution, effective planning and responsive action are vital to keep the university and its libraries in positions of national and world academic leadership. Accordingly, priority attention must be given to planning and action with respect to the human resources of the libraries of Columbia University. Attention should focus on:

- The staff required to lead, plan, and conduct the work of the libraries
- The relationships that should prevail between the libraries and

(1) the faculty and students, (2) the administration and other components of the university, and (3) other libraries and universities

- The relationships that should prevail among the members of the staff of Columbia's libraries
- The functions and responsibilities that should be assigned to library executives and supervisors

This chapter describes the libraries of Columbia University today. Subsequent chapters set forth plans for the future development of the libraries' human resources, organization and staffing, and approach to management and professional activities.

COLUMBIA UNIVERSITY

Columbia University in the City of New York presently comprises the Columbia Corporation and a number of affiliated institutions. The Columbia Corporation is governed by its Board of Trustees, led by the President, and includes sixteen undergraduate, graduate, and professional faculties. Undergraduate faculties are those of Columbia College and the School of General Studies. (Undergraduate degrees are also offered by the School of Engineering and Applied Sciences.) Graduate degree programs are the responsibility of the Graduate Schools of Arts and Sciences which consists of faculties of Political Science, Philosophy, and Pure Sciences. Professional programs are conducted by Schools of Architecture, Arts, Business, Dental and Oral Surgery, Engineering and Applied Sciences, International Affairs, Journalism, Law, Library Service, Medicine, and Social Work. There are seventy departments of instruction and forty-six interdisciplinary institutes, centers, and other project groupings within the Columbia Corporation. The affiliated institutions, each headed by its own governing board and president, are Barnard College, Teachers College, and the College of Pharmaceutical Sciences. Columbia University also has cooperative working relationships with many other institutions in the New York metropolitan area, the region, and the nation.

More than 16,000 students are enrolled at Columbia, as shown in Exhibit 2. Of these, 4,900 (30 percent) are in undergraduate programs, 6,700 (42 percent) are in professional schools, 2,900 (18 percent) are in the Graduate Schools of Arts and Sciences, and 1,600 (10 percent) are in special studies. Columbia's faculty includes more than 4,100 faculty members; staff members total about 7,300.

Columbia's Morningside campus is situated in a mixed socio-economic area on the upper West Side of Manhattan. The institution's facilities include some new, recently completed modern buildings; some old buildings long obsolete and confining; and many structures of different ages adapted to their present uses with various levels of effectiveness.

The university's operating budget charged against general income will total about $65.4 million for the 1971–1972 academic year. Columbia faces severe financial problems, however. The university has incurred an operating deficit every year since 1966–1967, and an operating deficit of about $12.8 million is estimated for 1971–1972.

The university's immediate financial goal is to eliminate its operating deficits by the 1973–1974 academic year by developing additional sources of financing and more funds from present sources. At the same time, however, the university will have to control and reduce costs, which in all likelihood will mean the restriction, reduction, and elimination of some academic and other programs. Thus, Columbia faces the extremely difficult task of having to maintain high academic standards and, at the same time, reduce operating deficits despite rapidly rising costs on every front. This financial challenge has major implications for Columbia's libraries and the need to strengthen the effectiveness and efficiency of their organization and staffing.

THE LIBRARIES OF COLUMBIA UNIVERSITY

The libraries of Columbia University have developed since 1763 to rank among the world's larger and more notable research libraries. They are vital to the continued excellence of the university's academic programs and to its ability to attract and retain the high-

EXHIBIT 2

COLUMBIA UNIVERSITY

ENROLLMENTS SERVED BY THE LIBRARIES
OF COLUMBIA UNIVERSITY

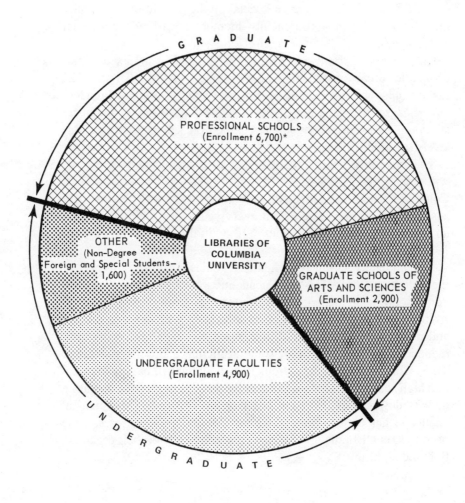

GRADUATE

PROFESSIONAL SCHOOLS
(Enrollment 6,700)*

OTHER
(Non-Degree
Foreign and Special Students—
1,600)

LIBRARIES OF
COLUMBIA
UNIVERSITY

GRADUATE SCHOOLS OF
ARTS AND SCIENCES
(Enrollment 2,900)

UNDERGRADUATE FACULTIES
(Enrollment 4,900)

UNDERGRADUATE

quality faculty and students it desires. More broadly, Columbia's libraries also include unique materials and collections which are an important part of man's accumulated intellectual resources and which serve scholars and professionals from many institutions and fields. Through participation in cooperative programs, associations, and interlibrary loans, Columbia's libraries are also an important element in a resource-sharing system among research libraries that is gradually being developed. Columbia will increasingly be called upon to contribute to—as well as being able to draw upon—this system as it becomes more institutionalized on a regional, national, and international basis.

The multiple relationships that the Columbia libraries maintain with Columbia Corporation, the affiliated institutions, and some of the many other organizations with which reciprocal ties are maintained are shown schematically in Exhibit 3.

Objectives of the Libraries

The Columbia libraries presently have no up-to-date formal statement of objectives. A number of aims are evident in practice, however, that give direction to the libraries' development and activities. Since the libraries are an integral part of Columbia, their objectives are intertwined with those of the university and essentially are to support the university's instructional and research programs. At the same time, because Columbia's libraries hold resources of regional, national, and international significance, they have objectives that transcend the university and make them part of the worldwide research library community.

A statement of Columbia's library objectives is set forth in Exhibit 4. It is interesting to note that the primary mission of securing, preserving, organizing, and deploying the information resources needed by the academic community requires that the libraries (1) relate their plans and priorities to those of the university, and (2) develop, organize, and effectively utilize the information and resource capabilities needed.

EXHIBIT 3

COLUMBIA UNIVERSITY

RELATIONSHIPS OF THE LIBRARIES OF COLUMBIA UNIVERSITY
TO THE UNIVERSITY, AFFILIATED INSTITUTIONS, AND OTHER ORGANIZATIONS

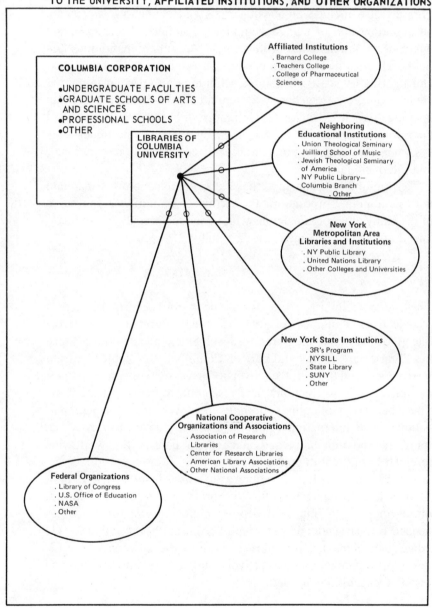

Affiliated Institutions
. Barnard College
. Teachers College
. College of Pharmaceutical
  Sciences

COLUMBIA CORPORATION

● UNDERGRADUATE FACULTIES
● GRADUATE SCHOOLS OF ARTS
  AND SCIENCES
● PROFESSIONAL SCHOOLS
● OTHER

**LIBRARIES OF
COLUMBIA
UNIVERSITY**

**Neighboring
Educational Institutions**
. Union Theological Seminary
. Juilliard School of Music
. Jewish Theological Seminary
  of America
. NY Public Library—
  Columbia Branch
          . Other

**New York
Metropolitan Area
Libraries and Institutions**
. NY Public Library
. United Nations Library
. Other Colleges and Universities

New York State Institutions
. 3R's Program
. NYSILL
. State Library
. SUNY
. Other

**National Cooperative
Organizations and Associations**
. Association of Research
  Libraries
. Center for Research Libraries
. American Library Associations
. Other National Associations

Federal Organizations
. Library of Congress
. U.S. Office of Education
. NASA
. Other

EXHIBIT 4

Columbia University

OBJECTIVES OF THE LIBRARIES OF
COLUMBIA UNIVERSITY

PURPOSE

The purpose of the Columbia University libraries is to acquire all forms of recorded information in selected fields pertinent to the goals of the university, and to make them available to members of the Columbia community engaged in research and study and in the pursuit of knowledge generally. The libraries also recognize their obligation to support the intellectual efforts of groups of scholars, students, and others outside the immediate university context in view of their unique capabilities nationally and internationally in areas of particular strength.

ROLE

The libraries of Columbia University strive to fulfill the purpose by (1) identifying and acquiring the resources in written material needed to support the instructional programs and individual and collective research efforts of Columbia's faculty and students, (2) making these resources available through central and specialized library units, and (3) assuring the security and condition of the collections.

PROGRAM OBJECTIVES

The following statements suggest overall and specific objectives the libraries of Columbia University seek to achieve in order to carry out their role effectively.

- To select and acquire those information resources most needed to support the research and instructional programs of Columbia University consistent with the objective of selective excellence
- To assure the continuing development directly or indirectly of those distinctive collection strengths that have been developed at Columbia, in recognition of the libraries' obligations as custodian of significant resources of regional, national, and international importance
- To make available readily to Columbia University faculty and students, and others as deemed appropriate, such materials as are needed, whether accessible immediately within present collections or from other collections on loan or by purchase
- To house library collections in facilities offering ready access to and usage of materials for circulation, reserve, and other purposes, and which are suitable for their preservation
- To maintain materials contained in Columbia's collections in excellent condition consistent with the need for accessibility to the user
- To assist the user to comprehend and utilize effectively library resources that are available immediately or that can be made available through other sources
- To offer library resources and services effectively and efficiently to maximize the utilization of the limited resources available
- To maintain close and meaningful working relationships with officials of the university and with academic departments and other official bodies to assure effective development of library resources consistent with university objectives and plans
- To maintain constructive working relationships with other research libraries, library associations, and cooperative organizations to enhance access to other resources and to effect the development of mutually advantageous approaches to collection policies' and interlibrary exchange

Collections

University use of and support for libraries have been unusually extensive at Columbia. The library collections have grown continuously since 1883 when various departmental libraries were consolidated into a single unified library system. By 1925, Columbia's collections had reached one million volumes. Today, just over forty-five years later, Columbia's collections exceed four million cataloged volumes.

Columbia's collections are not only large, but their quality, depth, and range are also exceptional in many areas such as architecture, library service, and East Asian and Slavic studies. In recent years, large files of technical reports, microforms, and other media have been incorporated in the collections in response to format changes. In addition, in technical service areas, efforts are being made to computerize bibliographic processing and to bring Columbia's records more closely in conformance with Library of Congress standards. The sizes and types of collections held in each of Columbia's eight library divisions by type of material are shown in Exhibits 5, 6, and 7.

The Columbia libraries also add to their own resources by cooperating in such efforts as the Center for Research Libraries, the New York Medical Library Center, and NYSILL. This cooperation provides convenient access to information resources available elsewhere in a variety of subject areas.

The growth rate of Columbia's collections has accelerated in recent years in response to the proliferation of published materials. From an average of fewer than 80,000 acquisitions annually prior to 1960, the acquisition rate has increased to over 130,000 volumes annually during the past decade, as shown in Exhibits 8 and 9. This increased rate has placed tremendous pressure on the technical services activity to handle the sheer volume of materials to be processed and increased demand for information.

Services to Users

Thirty-five decentralized operating units, organized in eight divisions, offer a variety of reference, circulation, and bibliographic

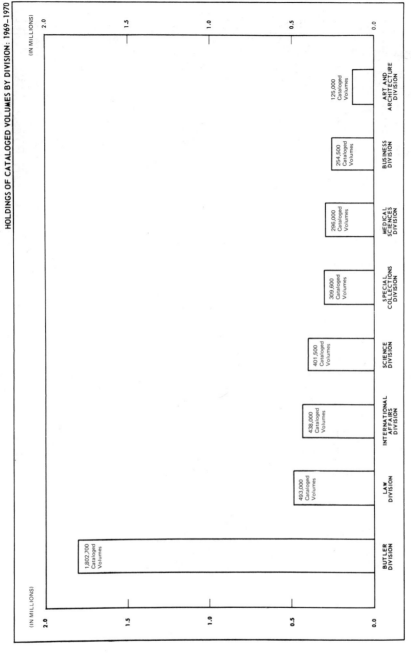

EXHIBIT 5

COLUMBIA UNIVERSITY

HOLDINGS OF CATALOGED VOLUMES BY DIVISION: 1969–1970

(IN MILLIONS)

2.0

1.5

1.0

0.5

0.0

BUTLER DIVISION — 1,802,700 Cataloged Volumes

LAW DIVISION — 493,000 Cataloged Volumes

INTERNATIONAL AFFAIRS DIVISION — 438,000 Cataloged Volumes

SCIENCE DIVISION — 401,500 Cataloged Volumes

SPECIAL COLLECTIONS DIVISION — 309,600 Cataloged Volumes

MEDICAL SCIENCES DIVISION — 296,000 Cataloged Volumes

BUSINESS DIVISION — 254,500 Cataloged Volumes

ART AND ARCHITECTURE DIVISION — 125,000 Cataloged Volumes

EXHIBIT 6

COLUMBIA UNIVERSITY

SERIAL SUBSCRIPTIONS BY DIVISION:
1969–1970

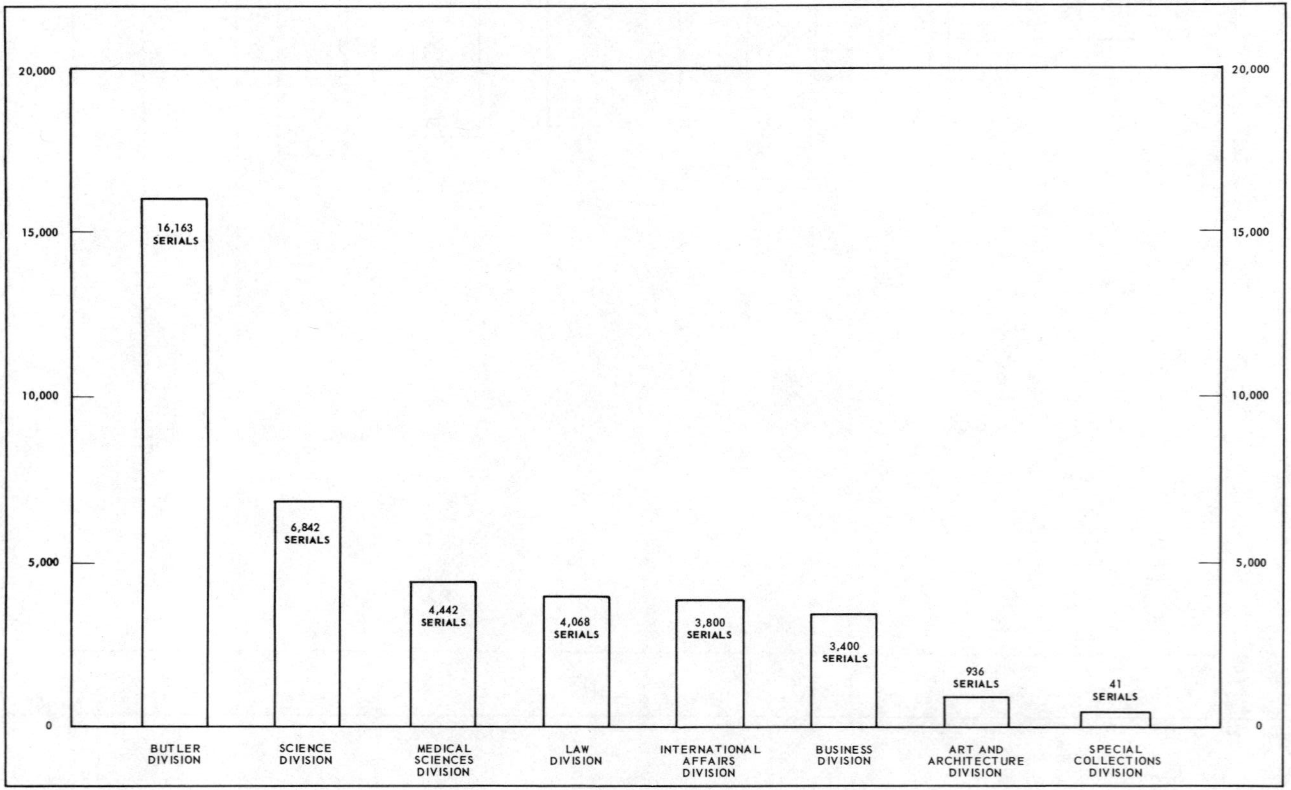

EXHIBIT 7

COLUMBIA UNIVERSITY

HOLDINGS OF SPECIALIZED MATERIALS:
1969–1970

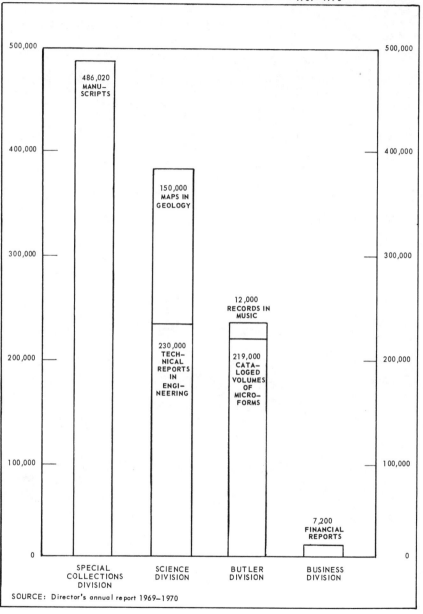

SOURCE: Director's annual report 1969–1970

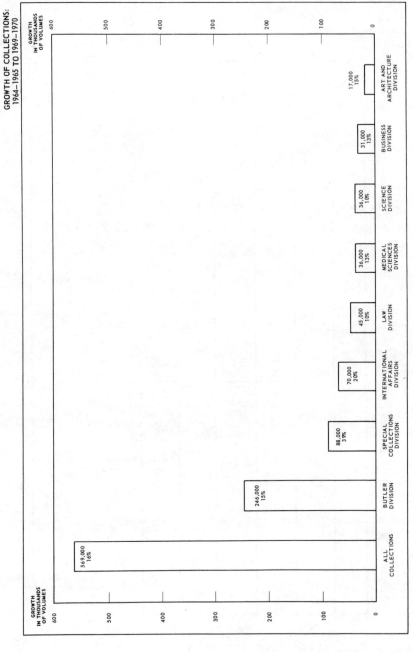

EXHIBIT 8

COLUMBIA UNIVERSITY

GROWTH OF COLLECTIONS:
1964–1965 TO 1969–1970

GROWTH
IN THOUSANDS
OF VOLUMES

ALL COLLECTIONS — 569,000 / 16%

BUTLER DIVISION — 246,000 / 15%

SPECIAL COLLECTIONS DIVISION — 88,000 / 3%

INTERNATIONAL AFFAIRS DIVISION — 70,000 / 20%

LAW DIVISION — 45,000 / 10%

MEDICAL SCIENCES DIVISION — 36,000 / 13%

SCIENCE DIVISION — 36,000 / 10%

BUSINESS DIVISION — 31,000 / 13%

ART AND ARCHITECTURE DIVISION — 17,000 / 15%

EXHIBIT 9

COLUMBIA UNIVERSITY

COLLECTION GROWTH AND NEW ACQUISITIONS:
1954–1955 TO 1969–1970

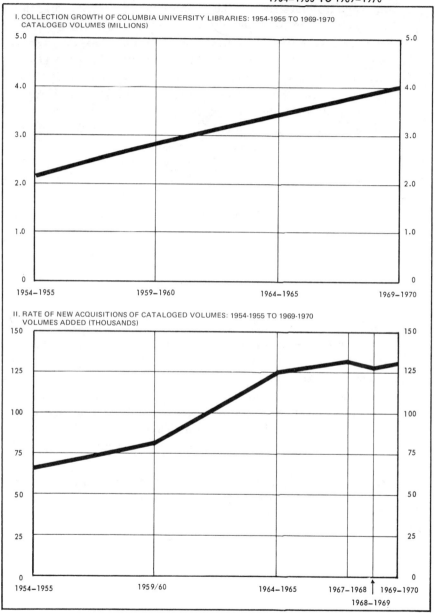

I. COLLECTION GROWTH OF COLUMBIA UNIVERSITY LIBRARIES: 1954-1955 TO 1969-1970
CATALOGED VOLUMES (MILLIONS)

II. RATE OF NEW ACQUISITIONS OF CATALOGED VOLUMES: 1954-1955 TO 1969-1970
VOLUMES ADDED (THOUSANDS)

services and serve distinctive groups. The Butler Division comprises the central library serving the entire university, particularly in the humanities. The Business Division and Columbia College Library offer reserve reading resources utilizing computers for inventory and bibliographic control. The Music, Engineering, and Geology Libraries and the Special Collections Division have developed specialized resources, such as records, documents, technical reports, and maps. Other units have created special capabilities, such as the news morgue in the Journalism Library and medical reference services in the Medical Sciences Division.

The user patterns of the eight library divisions at Columbia and an indication of the types of use made of library services are set forth in Exhibits 10 and 11.

Facilities

With the exception of the Medical Sciences Division, the operating libraries are located reasonably close together on Columbia's Morningside campus shown on the map in Exhibit 12. This proximity allows users convenient access to a wide variety of library resources and facilitates working relationships among library staff.

Because Columbia is situated in an urban community, there are practical limits on physical expansion. This physical constraint, coupled with severe financial limitations, prevents the building of much needed new facilities. As a result, plans for an instructional resources center, proper reading and storage facilities for special collections, a centralized science collection, a social work library facility, and renovation of Butler have been postponed or cancelled. The fact that only four of the thirty-five operating units (Business, Engineering, Law, and International Affairs) are considered adequate or modern illustrates the dimensions of Columbia's facility limitations.

EXHIBIT 10

COLUMBIA UNIVERSITY

CHARACTERISTICS OF LIBRARY DIVISIONS
IN TERMS OF RELATIVE SIZE OF COLLECTIONS
AND USER PATTERNS

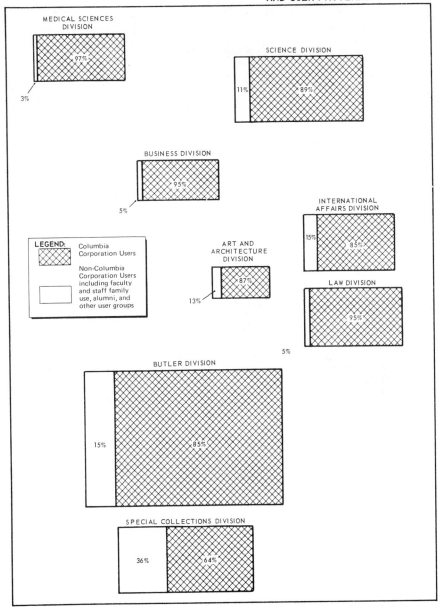

EXHIBIT 11

COLUMBIA UNIVERSITY

USE OF LIBRARIES BY TYPE OF USER AND SERVICE OR RESOURCE USED*

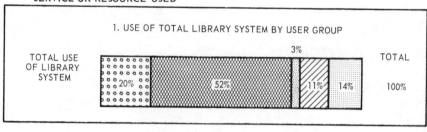

1. USE OF TOTAL LIBRARY SYSTEM BY USER GROUP

TOTAL USE OF LIBRARY SYSTEM — 20% — 52% — 3% — 11% — 14% — TOTAL 100%

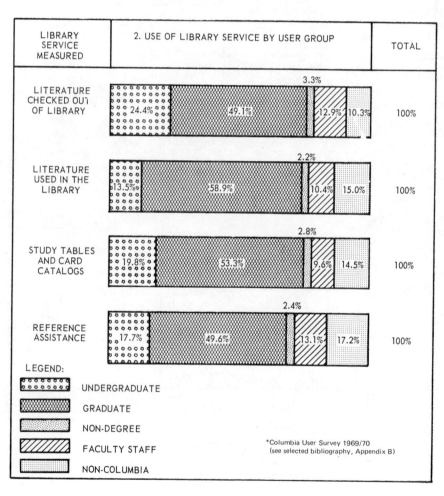

LIBRARY SERVICE MEASURED	2. USE OF LIBRARY SERVICE BY USER GROUP	TOTAL
LITERATURE CHECKED OUT OF LIBRARY	24.4% — 49.1% — 3.3% — 12.9% — 10.3%	100%
LITERATURE USED IN THE LIBRARY	13.5% — 58.9% — 2.2% — 10.4% — 15.0%	100%
STUDY TABLES AND CARD CATALOGS	19.8% — 53.3% — 2.8% — 9.6% — 14.5%	100%
REFERENCE ASSISTANCE	17.7% — 49.6% — 2.4% — 13.1% — 17.2%	100%

LEGEND:

- UNDERGRADUATE
- GRADUATE
- NON-DEGREE
- FACULTY STAFF
- NON-COLUMBIA

*Columbia User Survey 1969/70
(see selected bibliography, Appendix B)

EXHIBIT 12

COLUMBIA UNIVERSITY

MAP OF COLUMBIA UNIVERSITY CAMPUS

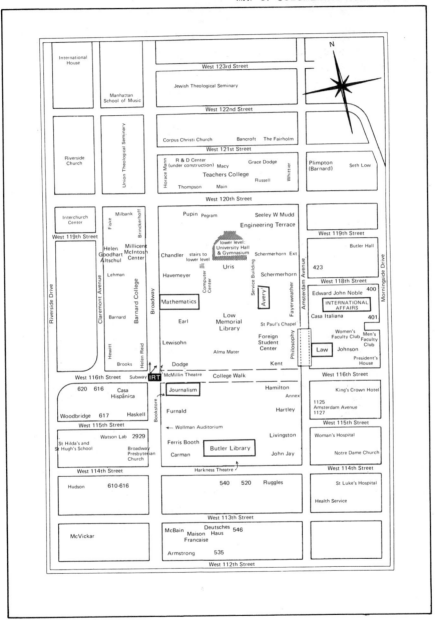

The libraries of Columbia are under the leadership of the Director of Libraries and include thirty-five operating units organized in eight divisions.

Director of Libraries

The Director of Libraries provides overall leadership in the development of the academic services offered by the divisions and operating units, and oversees administrative and technical services that support the system as a whole. By university statute, the Director of Libraries is the chief executive officer of all libraries, appointed by and accountable to the President through the Executive Vice President for Academic Affairs and Provost. His responsibilities are to:

- Implement university statutes pertinent to the libraries
- Study continuously needs and conditions of the libraries and report on these from time to time to the President
- Appoint all staff and establish titles, duties, and compensation
- Control the use of all library buildings, rooms, equipment, and other properties
- Make and implement rules relating to the use of the libraries and their resources, with the approval of the President

The Director of Libraries is assisted by a deputy, the Associate Director, who is responsible for coordination of library academic services provided through the several divisions. In addition, there are three other offices providing central services:

- *Office of the Associate Director for Technical Services*—Responsible for acquisitions, materials preservation, and bibliographic records processing
- *Office of the Assistant Director for Administrative Services* —Responsible for (1) professional and nonprofessional personnel, (2) fiscal control, and (3) library privileges, space utilization, security, and equipment
- *Library Systems Office*—Responsible for the development of systems design and computer applications

Administrative Structure

Columbia's libraries are organized in eight divisions consisting of thirty-five operating units, as reflected in Exhibit 13. The Butler Division consists of the central university library serving undergraduate, graduate, and faculty research needs. The remaining divisions consist of one or more operating library units serving specific graduate or professional schools and particular aspects of the sciences.

The management dynamics at the Columbia libraries are only partially conveyed by the organization chart. An important objective of library leadership is to get staff constructively involved in solving library problems. Eight standing committees have been active over the past year in considering specific matters of importance to the libraries and advising the Director on actions needed. The areas under discussion have been computer applications, collection development and preservation, content and form of bibliographic records, supporting staff classification, general services, and interinstitutional relations, humanistic and historical research services, and science research services. In addition, a Representative Committee of Librarians concerned largely with professional questions is elected by professional staff members.

STAFFING PATTERNS

Current staffing levels at the Columbia libraries for each division and administrative unit are shown in Exhibit 14. Total staff size has grown 80 percent over the past sixteen years from 311 in 1955 to 345 in 1960 to the present budgeted level of 559. This growth has been rather evenly distributed among all the divisions, except, of course, for the newly formed International Affairs Division.

A characteristic of the changing staff patterns is the greater use of paraprofessional and clerical personnel. This is most apparent in the Office for Technical Services where in 1955 the ratio of professional to nonprofessional staff was almost 1 : 1, while today professionals are outnumbered almost 2.5 : 1. For the libraries as a whole, the ratio of professional to nonprofessional staff has

EXHIBIT 13
COLUMBIA UNIVERSITY
PRESENT PLAN OF ORGANIZATION

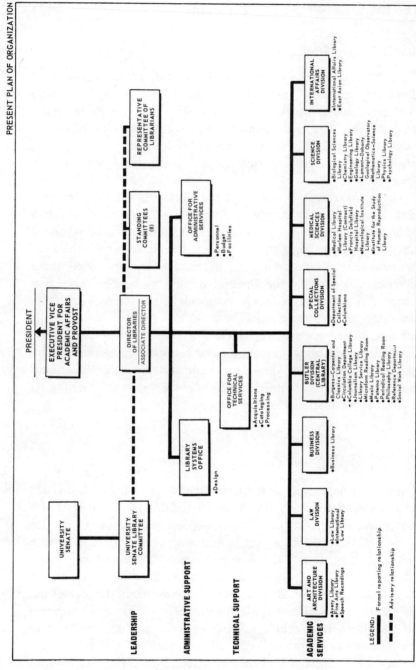

EXHIBIT 14

COLUMBIA UNIVERSITY

DISTRIBUTION OF BUDGETED STAFF POSITIONS:
1969–1970

SPECIAL COLLECTIONS DIVISION — 6.5 / 9

ART AND ARCHITECTURE DIVISION — 7 / 9

BUSINESS DIVISION — 6 / 20

LAW DIVISION — 8 / 24

MEDICAL SCIENCES DIVISION — 14 / 23.5

SCIENCE DIVISION — 9 / 29

INTERNATIONAL AFFAIRS DIVISION — 19.5 / 23

CENTRAL ADMINISTRATION — 19 / 25.5

BUTLER DIVISION — 22 / 98.5

OFFICE FOR TECHNICAL SERVICES — 54.5 / 128

LEGEND:

PROFESSIONAL

NONPROFESSIONAL

TOTAL PROFESSIONAL AND NONPROFESSIONAL
(1969-1970) - 559

also changed, though not so dramatically, from 0.67 : 1 in 1955 to 0.50 : 1 in 1970, or about two nonprofessionals for each professional library staff member.

This changing staff pattern reflects several factors, including (1) a response to a difficult labor market, (2) refinement of professional job content, (3) growing specialization in the processing activities, (4) accommodation to the expanding work load within tight budget constraints, and (5) the changing nature of technical services demonstrated by the increasing use of Library of Congress cataloging information and the application of computerized techniques.

LIBRARY EXPENDITURES

Columbia's total library expenditures increased more than threefold over the past decade from $1.8 million in 1959–1960 to $5.9 million in 1969–1970. Currently, 67 percent of total expenditures is for salaries and wages, 28 percent for books, serials, and bindings, and 5 percent for supplies and miscellaneous. Over the past five years, personnel replaced books as the most rapidly rising cost to the libraries, as shown in the table on page below.

COMPARISON OF EXPENDITURES BY CATEGORY
1959–1960 to 1969–1970

				Percent Increase	
	1959–1960	1964–1965	1969–1970	1959–1964	1964–1969
	(Dollars in Thousands)				
Salaries and wages	$1,283	$2,184	$4,000	69%	82%
Books, serials, and bindings	441	998	1,649	150	60
Supplies and miscellaneous	102	207	304	102	50
Total	$1,826	$3,389	$5,953	89%	76%

EXHIBIT 15

COLUMBIA UNIVERSITY

DISTRIBUTION OF OPERATING BUDGET:
1970–1971

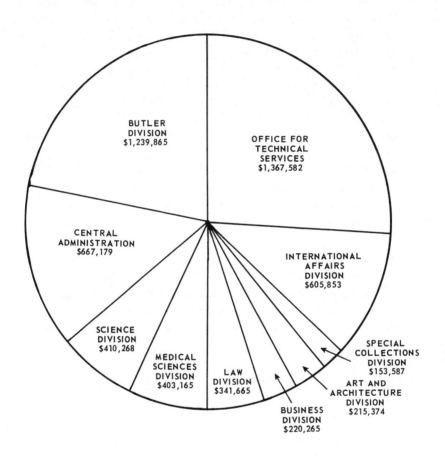

BUTLER
DIVISION
$1,239,865

OFFICE FOR
TECHNICAL
SERVICES
$1,367,582

CENTRAL
ADMINISTRATION
$667,179

INTERNATIONAL
AFFAIRS
DIVISION
$605,853

SCIENCE
DIVISION
$410,268

SPECIAL
COLLECTIONS
DIVISION
$153,587

MEDICAL
SCIENCES
DIVISION
$403,165

LAW
DIVISION
$341,665

ART AND
ARCHITECTURE
DIVISION
$215,374

BUSINESS
DIVISION
$220,265

The distribution of the current budget among the several library components is shown in Exhibit 15. As depicted in this exhibit, 29 percent of the total current budget is for technical services, 25 percent for the Butler Division or central library, 11 percent for central administration, and the balance, or 35 percent, for the other seven library divisions.

Currently, due to the severe financial pressures facing the university, the Columbia library budget allocation from general funds for the academic year 1971–1972 is only 5 percent more than the 1970–1971 budget. In fact, in view of both the rising acquisition and personnel costs and the declining funds from nonuniversity sources, Columbia's libraries face an actual decline in the resources available.

An important function of the central library administration is budget preparation and control. Professional salaries and acquisitions, in particular, are scrutinized and limits are established by the director's office in consultation with division officers subject to the total budget allocation. Overseeing and coordinating budget implementation are also central administration responsibilities.

The characteristics of the libraries of Columbia University have been reviewed briefly in this chapter to provide a perspective in which to view the organization and staffing recommendations outlined in Chapters II and III.

CHAPTER TWO

Recommended Plan
of Organization

The ability of Columbia University's libraries to meet the challenges and demands of the future—to achieve their objectives, to build and maintain outstanding collections, and to provide programs and services vital to the university and society—will be determined largely by the way in which the libraries' human resources are organized to work together. The plan of organization recommended in this chapter should enhance the capacity of Columbia University's libraries to perform effectively in the decade ahead.

The need for reorganization of Columbia's libraries is fundamental. Knowledge is proliferating at an unprecedented rate, new modes of transmitting and recording information are available, and traditional disciplines are being subdivided into new specialties and blurred by interdisciplinary pursuits. The impact of these trends is manifest in the growing size, diversity, and complexity of library information resources and in the increased difficulty for faculty and students alike of drawing upon these resources effectively. As a result, research libraries more than ever before will need to develop more sophisticated capabilities to help the academic community obtain, gain access to, and draw upon the recorded information available to meet their research and instruction needs. At the same time that new levels of sophistication will be reached among some

37

user groups, beginning users will find the libraries increasingly complex and incomprehensible.

The present general plan of organization at Columbia is ill-equipped to develop needed service capabilities. This plan has been developed largely to administer library components as self-contained operations with executive professional staff responsible for a wide variety of academic service and resource areas. As a result, professional efforts are often spread thinly among many operating demands which inhibits development of specialized capabilities. Unless change is made, staff will increasingly be burdened with pressures for specialized user services they are unable to meet.

The plan of organization recommended in this chapter is geared to building service capabilities along two essential lines: (1) facilitating basic understanding of and access to library resources and services by all users (i.e., the services function) and (2) gaining full advantage for sophisticated users of complex information sources by making available specialized subject-competent professional capabilities (i.e., the resources function). Staffing patterns matched to the recommended organization plan are provided in Chapter III. Management approaches are suggested in Chapter IV.

REQUIREMENTS OF ORGANIZATION

The organization plan adopted for Columbia's research libraries should be geared to trends in higher education and to management principles.

Trends in Higher Education

Columbia's libraries should be organized in light of major trends in higher education and their implications for the organization and staffing of libraries, cited in Appendix A. Evaluating these trends leads to the conclusion that the organization of Columbia's libraries has lagged significantly. There is need for responsive information programs to meet a wider range of instructional and research requirements than ever before. Changing fields of interests and disciplines make it apparent that the research library can no longer continue to mirror the academic programs of the university; this strategy is too expensive and difficult to keep up to date.

Columbia's centralized organization is well suited for coordinated program development, administration, and control. The present organization needs substantial strengthening, however, to be able to develop the professional service capabilities that will be required to keep pace with emerging fields and approaches to instruction and research, to assist faculty in curriculum planning, to provide backup instructional and reference assistance to students, and to maintain selective and meaningful control over collection priorities. In addition, the sheer volume of additions to Columbia's collections in the future and the growing academic need for access to information across subject fields will make it doubly important for the libraries to facilitate user access to their expanding resources.

A major drawback to the present plan is that the organization is primarily geared to administering thirty-five different libraries as self-contained operating units. This is fully effective only when users come to the libraries fully understanding their needs and having a good idea of the library resources available. Library efforts under the present plan therefore tend to become more concerned with such questions as physical access to and the security of the collections than with helping members of the academic community meet their current awareness needs and obtain the information and professional assistance needed to make their instructional and research activities truly effective. Thus, the organization tends to be rather rigid and not dynamic or flexible enough to develop specialized services that can be provided as needed.

The result of this organizational pattern is the deployment of valuable professional staff resources largely for purposes of administrative supervision and control, with inadequate provision for developing subject, bibliographic, research, and other professional competencies that could readily be used by the academic community. The structure and staff are more oriented to management and day-to-day operations than to critical functional areas or information problems that cut across administrative lines and that could result in substantial improvements in sophisticated services available to the university community.

Organization Principles

Principles that should be observed in organization planning have been identified through management analysis and experience over the years. Some principles are applicable in human enterprises generally. Others are applicable primarily in enterprises with particular types of objectives—such as the orientation of businesses to profit, health enterprises to patient care, and educational institutions to teaching, research, and community service. Columbia's libraries should be organized in accordance with organization principles applicable in the university research library field.

The present plan of library organization at Columbia is consistent with many of these management principles. The libraries benefit from system-wide leadership and coordination under a single director. The operating units are organized in divisions for administrative efficiency and professional leadership. In several respects, however, the present organization of Columbia's libraries should be strengthened. Valuable professional staff resources are presently spread thinly among a wide span of activities. This approach develops generalist administrative talents and offers flexibility in that staff can be readily shifted from one area to another. At the same time, however, this administrative orientation means that staff are less well able to develop specialized instructional, reference, research, and other sophisticated skills needed at a university. As a result, librarians have difficulty in building on their own special training and interests and in providing improved levels of professional service through extended experience.

PROPOSED OVERALL APPROACH TO ORGANIZATION FOR
COLUMBIA UNIVERSITY LIBRARIES

Columbia University should now adopt a plan of organization for its libraries to prepare them to meet the needs of the future. The plan adopted should providefor:

- The university libraries to continue to be organized on a centralized basis

- The libraries to be headed by a single general executive officer with the title of Vice President and University Librarian
- The libraries to be organized internally in five major units that are mutually interdependent and work together closely and cooperatively
- A few libraries, namely the Law Library Center, the Medical Science Information Center, and the distinctive collections, to continue to report directly to the Vice President and University Librarian
- Working relationships to be clarified and strengthened between the university libraries and both the university administration and the faculties

These features are the essential elements of the recommended plan. Each is important to the success and effectiveness of the university libraries. The overall plan of organization is shown in Exhibit 16. The sections which follow describe in detail the plan's components.

Continued Centralized Organization

Columbia University, along with a few other institutions, is notable among major American universities in that its libraries have been organized on a centralized basis for decades. The university statutes provide that:

- "There shall be a director of libraries . . . who shall be the general executive officer of all libraries under the control of the university." (Ch. VIII, ¶ 80)
- "The director of libraries shall appoint all needed assistants and subordinate officers. . . ." (Ch. VIII, ¶ 81)
- "The designation 'librarian' shall apply only to an officer appointed as such. . . ." (Ch. VIII, ¶ 82)
- "All books . . . and other printed matter given to the university or purchased . . . shall be deemed a part of the libraries . . . and all such purchases shall be made by the libraries. . . ." (Ch. VIII, ¶ 83)

EXHIBIT 16

COLUMBIA UNIVERSITY

RECOMMENDED OVERALL PLAN OF ORGANIZATION

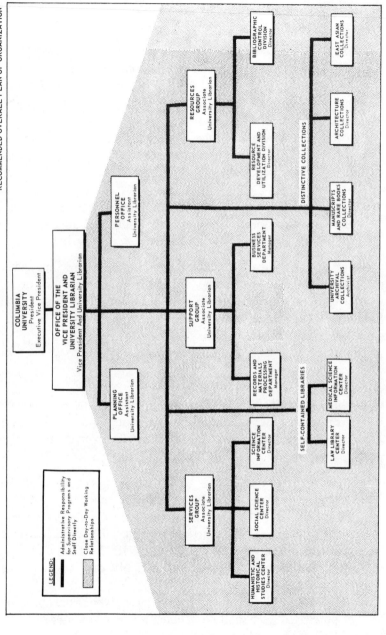

Whether it continues to be desirable for the Columbia libraries to be organized on a centralized basis was a major question addressed in the study. University libraries in America tend to be organized either along highly centralized or partially decentralized lines. Each of the two basic models has its own strengths and weaknesses which were evaluated in light of Columbia's requirements. Briefly, the characteristics of each system can be highlighted as follows.

- *A Highly Centralized System*—Under the highly centralized university-wide system, the university libraries may or may not be centralized physically. Such a system is characterized by:

  —The existence of a single university librarian as director of libraries with a central administrative support staff
  —Central planning, policy formulation and enforcement, budget formulation and control, and personnel administration
  —All librarians (including those serving professional schools) ultimately responsible to the single university librarian or director of libraries, even where activities are geographically decentralized

  Columbia University is one of a few institutions now organized on this basis.

- *A Partially Decentralized System*—A partially decentralized system has many of the characteristics of the fully centralized system, but significant exceptions are made for a few specialized libraries, such as those serving schools of law and medicine, which operate as relatively autonomous entities. This partially decentralized system is characterized by:

  —A principal university library or group of libraries that serves the academic community as a whole, responsible to a university librarian or director of libraries
  —One or more libraries that are not part of the library system and that:

    - May be responsible to deans or university officials other than the university librarian
    - May operate under budgets separate from the one for which the university librarian is responsible

EXHIBIT 17

COLUMBIA UNIVERSITY

ALTERNATIVE WAYS IN WHICH UNIVERSITY
LIBRARIES MIGHT BE ORGANIZED

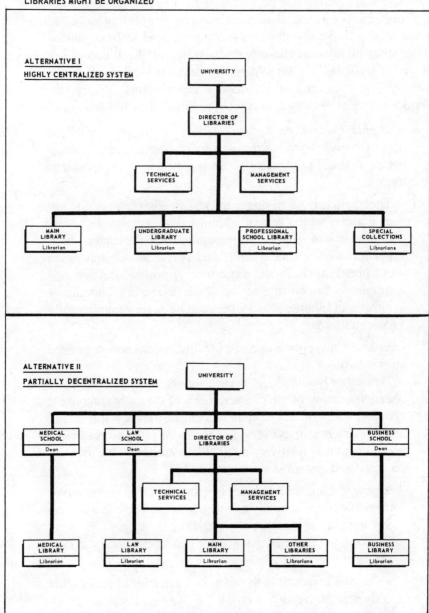

- May or may not be responsible for technical services in support of their own collections
- May or may not be available for use by the general academic community

This is the pattern of organization that, with variations, is in use at most American universities.

A chart of each alternative is presented in Exhibit 17.

A centralized plan of organization for the Columbia libraries will continue to meet the institution's total needs more effectively than the other major alternative or its possible variations. There are many persuasive reasons for continuing the centralized plan at Columbia. It offers real advantages in coordinating the development of library resources in accordance with university priorities. The plan has the advantage of maintaining the status of the libraries and enhancing their capacity to represent library concerns and needs effectively before university officials. The central approach also offers benefits in minimizing overlap and duplication and in developing specialized capabilities needed to serve the diverse needs of the academic community. Exhibit 18 presents a summary evaluation of each alternative. The centralized plan has proven to be extremely successful at Columbia. There is every reason to believe that this plan could be applied with benefit at other institutions.

Vice President and University Librarian

Columbia's libraries have long been headed by a single general executive who has held the title of Director of Libraries. In recent years, he has reported to the Executive Vice President for Academic Affairs and Provost.

For the future, it is proposed that the senior library executive have the title of Vice President and University Librarian. This seems entirely appropriate in view of:

- The major and increasing responsibility this individual is assigned as a general officer of the university
- The need for him to work as a peer with other senior members of the university's administration in planning for the university

EXHIBIT 18

Columbia University

EVALUATION OF ALTERNATIVE WAYS IN WHICH
UNIVERSITY LIBRARIES MIGHT BE ORGANIZED

Centralized

Potential Advantages	Potential Disadvantages
. Assures coordination of library development for the university as a whole.	. Increases distance from primary user groups.
. Elevates the status of the library and enhances its capacity to represent library concerns and needs before central university officials.	. Loses sight of unique features of different collections or of different user group requirements by oversimplification.
. Helps avoid unnecessary duplication in collection development and service activities.	. Hampers efforts to gain funding support from different departments and schools that under this system are less directly responsible for supporting library development.
. Facilitates the allocation of limited financial and manpower resources among the various libraries according to priority needs.	. Can attract unfavorable attention to the total costs of university libraries without the buffer of schools and departments interceding on behalf of the libraries as they might under another system.
. Places responsibility for implementing university priorities in the hands of central professional library leadership, rather than leaving execution to academic, administrative, and other officials who may not be well prepared or knowledgeable about library needs as in a decentralized scheme.	. Increases the problems of relating library expenditures to concrete services provided to distinct user groups.
. Permits the development of system-wide specialized services that individual operating units typically could not afford.	. Can exaggerate the performance of specific functions for their own sake by virtue of size and functional specialization.
. Broadens the career opportunities for professional staff by (1) bringing together all library activities in a single system and (2) encouraging specialization to occur by drawing on professional talents and interests.	

Partially Decentralized

Potential Advantages	Potential Disadvantages
. Allows the development of a large centralized resource center which serves as research and collection backup for branch libraries.	. Has many of the limitations listed for centralized systems as well as other difficulties.
. Attempts to gain the strengths of department libraries, such as relationships with faculties, convenience of collections, and sophistication of services.	. Inhibits the system's capacity to develop sophisticated reader and other services that can be made available to all operating units.
	. Limits the university's capacity to evaluate, for example, collection development priorities among the main libraries and other units. Encourages duplication.
	. Encourages the development of costly library collections, staff, and facilities for each new or existing school or department as a matter of precedent and status.

and its libraries on an integrated basis, and in formulating
and enforcing a major budget and policies of significance to
all or most elements of the university

- The need for him to work closely with and represent the university administration to the faculty, the faculty senate, and senate
committees
- The magnitude of his responsibilities measured in terms of:

—The importance and size of library collections and library
programs and services
—The number of library staff members to whom he must provide professional leadership and executive directions
—The size of the operating budget for which he is responsible

- The need for him to represent the university at highest levels
on a broad basis to:

—Other universities
—Scholarly organizations
—Professional organizations
—Cooperative organizations in the library field
—Federal, state, and local government agencies
—Other organizations

The libraries are a vital and integral part of Columbia. Under
the recommended plan of organization, the Vice President and
University Librarian should be regarded as part of the university's
top administration. The President and Executive Vice President
for Academic Affairs and Provost should regard him as a member
of the university's key management team, a member of their
immediate staff, and a member of the presidential cabinet. The
Vice President and University Librarian should also regard himself
as a member of top management responsible for providing executive
direction to the libraries as a critical component of the university's
total resources. He should relate to the other vice presidents of
the university as a peer and a co-responsible member of the executive
group. Exhibit 19 reflects the relationships that should prevail.

The Vice President and University Librarian should be responsible
directly to the Executive Vice President for Academic Affairs and
Provost. He should take continuing direction from the Executive
Vice President. At the same time, he should provide advice, counsel,

EXHIBIT 19

COLUMBIA UNIVERSITY

RECOMMENDED RELATIONSHIPS BETWEEN THE LIBRARIES AND THE UNIVERSITY ADMINISTRATION AND FACULTIES

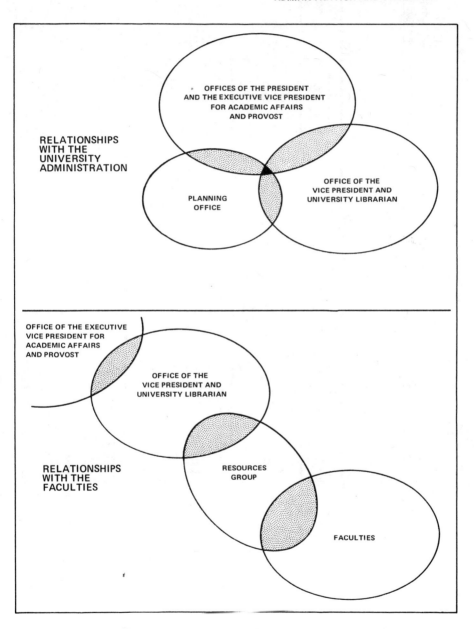

EXHIBIT 20

COLUMBIA UNIVERSITY

RECOMMENDED PLAN OF COMMITTEE RELATIONSHIPS

LEGEND:
— Administrative reporting relationship
■ ■ ■ Committee advisory relationship

COLUMBIA UNIVERSITY
President
Executive Vice President

OFFICE OF THE VICE PRESIDENT AND UNIVERSITY LIBRARIAN
Vice President And University Librarian

UNIVERSITY SENATE LIBRARY COMMITTEE

PROFESSIONAL ADVISORY COMMITTEE

TASK FORCES

STAFF DEVELOPMENT COMMITTEE

REPRESENTATIVE COMMITTEE OF LIBRARIANS

PLANNING OFFICE
Assistant University Librarian

TECHNICAL ADVISORY GROUPS

PERSONNEL OFFICE
Assistant University Librarian

TECHNICAL ADVISORY GROUPS

SUPPORT GROUP
Associate University Librarian

TECHNICAL ADVISORY GROUPS

SERVICES GROUP
Associate University Librarian

PROGRAM ADVISORY GROUPS

TECHNICAL ADVISORY GROUPS

RESOURCES GROUP
Associate University Librarian

PROGRAM ADVISORY GROUPS

TECHNICAL ADVISORY GROUPS

and staff assistance to the Executive Vice President and the President on both library and general university matters.

Committees and Advisory Groups

Within and related to Columbia's libraries, there should be formally organized committees and advisory groups. These are essential to conduct the ongoing work of the libraries and to provide a strong, effective approach to management and professional activities. These groups should also provide library staff members and faculty members who wish to do so with opportunities to participate in and contribute to the work of the libraries.

To meet anticipated needs at Columbia, it is recommended that:

- The present University Senate Library Committee be continued without change in its functions or composition
- The Representative Committee of Librarians be continued but that it not be assigned specialized tasks which might detract from its basic purpose
- A major Professional Advisory Committee be established to be concerned comprehensively with the work of the libraries at Columbia
- A Staff Development Committee be established to advise on and participate in the staff development activities proposed in Chapter IV
- Program advisory groups and technical advisory groups be appointed by unit heads to assist them in their work

Specific committees and advisory groups that should be appointed are shown in Exhibit 20. Exhibit 21 provides more detailed information about each proposed group, and sets forth the overall organization and committee structure.

PROPOSED ADMINISTRATIVE ORGANIZATION

Within the libraries of Columbia University, in addition to the office of the Vice President and University Librarian, there should be

EXHIBIT 21 (1)

Columbia University

RECOMMENDED COMMITTEE RESPONSIBILITIES
AND CHARACTERISTICS

Unit	Responsibilities	Work Assignments Made by:	Number of Members
University Senate Library Committee	. To "review and recommend university policies relating to the university libraries so as to advance the role of the libraries in the effectuation of the university's educational purposes." . To "work with the libraries, the president and the trustees to effectuate such policies." . (Established by the By-Laws, Statutes, and Rules of the Columbia University Senate, Section 3 (f) (12).) . To "report recommendations for consideration and action by the senate as a whole." (Section 3 (c).)	. Committee initiative	13 Total . 4 tenured faculty . 1 nontenured faculty . 3 students . 1 administration . 3 library staff . 1 research staff
Professional Advisory Committee	. To provide comprehensive professional advice and counsel to the Vice President and University Librarian. . To conduct specific studies in professional areas, usually through appointment of a task force. . To provide comprehensive advice and counsel to the Planning Office.	. Vice President and University Librarian	12 Total . Professional library staff . Faculty members with outstanding qualifications
Task Forces	. To conduct specific studies assigned by the Professional Advisory Committee. . To report findings and recommendations to the Professional Advisory Committee.	. Chairman of the Professional Advisory Committee with the concurrence of the Vice President and University Librarian	3-10 Total . Professional library staff . Specialist and clerical library staff . Faculty members . Students . Others
Representative Committee of Librarians	. To consider matters of concern to librarians. To discuss these informally with the Vice President and University Librarian. . To receive informal reports of library plans, progress, and problems from the Vice President and University Librarian. To discuss these informally.	. Committee initiative . Request of the Vice President and University Librarian	7 Total . Elected members of the professional staff

Members Selected by:	Duration of Assignment	Comment
. Election by the Senate on nomination of the Executive Committee of the Senate	. Continuing	. Is a committee of the university Senate rather than of the libraries
. Appointment by the Vice President and University Librarian . Library staff members generally selected from a panel of names developed by the Representative Committee of Librarians . Chairman appointed by the Vice President and University Librarian	. Continuing . Specific assignments to be completed within designated time period	. Is the senior professional committee of the libraries . Most matters of professional significance should be submitted to it for study and/or review prior to action on the part of the Vice President and University Librarian
. Appointment by the Chairman of the Professional Advisory Committee with the concurrence of the Vice President and University Librarian . Chairman appointed by the Chairman of the Professional Advisory Committee	. Specified, limited time period within which assignment is to be completed . Task force discharged upon completion of assignment	. A number of task forces will be at work at any one time . Work assignments may be given in any professional or technical area . Size and membership of the task force should be determined by assignment . Written assignment instructions and time period should be provided . Written reports should be required . Composition of task forces should include at least one beginning professional
. Election by librarians . Chairman elected by committee	. Continuing	. Acts as ombudsman for individual librarians . Committee and Vice President and University Librarian should meet monthly . Meetings should be informal with a free two-way exchange of views . Committee should rarely be asked to undertake specific work assignments

EXHIBIT 21 (2)

Unit	Responsibilities	Work Assignments Made by:	Number of Members
Staff Development Committee	. To review and recommend adoption of staff development plans. . To review performance of individual professional staff members on a periodic, scheduled basis. . To recommend steps to advance professional development.	. Request of Vice President and University Librarian and/or Assistant University Librarian for Personnel	3-5 Total . Professional library staff members
Program Advisory Groups	. To provide comprehensive advice and counsel on program matters to Associate University Librarians. . To conduct specific program studies and recommend action.	. Request of the Associate University Librarians	3-10 Total . Library staff members . Faculty members . Students . Others
Technical Advisory Groups	. To provide advice and counsel on technical matters. . To conduct specific technical studies and recommend action.	. Request of the Associate or Assistant University Librarians	3-10 Total . Library staff members . Faculty members . Students . Others

Members Selected by:	Duration of Assignment	Comment

. Appointment by the Vice President and University Librarian
. Members generally selected from a panel of names developed by the Representative Committee of Librarians
. Chairman appointed by the Vice President and University Librarian
. Members generally senior professional staff members who do not have major administrative assignments
	. Continuing	. Committee to meet at least monthly to review performance of professional staff members on a scheduled basis
		. Staff members to be reviewed:
		  - Every six months during first two years
		  - Annually during third to tenth year
		  - Every two years after the tenth year
		. Assistant University Librarian for Personnel to provide staff assistance and serve as Secretary of committee

. Appointment by the Associate University Librarians . Composition based on work assigned . Chairmen designated by Associate University Librarians	. Continuing or for specific time period at the option of the Associate University Librarians	. Associate University Librarian heading each group appoints program advisory groups at his initiative . Work assignments may be general or specific
. Appointment by the Associate or Assistant University Librarians . Composition based on work assigned . Chairmen designated by Associate or Assistant University Librarians	. Specific, limited time period within which assignment is to be completed	. Each Associate or Assistant University Librarian appoints technical advisory groups he wishes . Work assignments may be given in any technical area . Size and composition of group should be determined by assignment . Written assignment instructions and time schedule should be provided

five major organization units. These units, shown earlier in Exhibit 16, should be the:

Planning Office   }   Two system-wide staff offices that support and are intimately re-
Personnel Office   lated to the office of the Vice President and University Librarian

Services Group
Support Group   }   Three large mutually interdependent units with major operating
Resources Group   responsibilities

In addition, also reporting directly to the Vice President and University Librarian are the Law Library Center, the Medical Science Information Center, and the distinctive collections. These libraries, for reasons set forth later, are not appropriately within the Resources and Services Groups, although they are fully integrated components of the entire system.

The recommended plan is a significant departure from the present plan in use at Columbia and at other universities' libraries. The traditional division of activities between (1) reader or user services and (2) technical services is not followed. Rather, all activities are redistributed, expanded in concept, and enhanced in emphasis. This is especially true with respect to the resources area where it is proposed that professional work be heavily concentrated.

It should be noted that in the recommended plan the:

Services Group will include a few professional staff members and many technical and support staff members, will serve library users on a day-to-day basis, and will . . .

Operate service centers (bringing together existing small service units) that will:

- Serve library users' immediate needs
- Provide first-line information and referral services
- Provide self-service access to library collections
- Provide ready reference assistance

Resources Group will comprise primarily professional staff, will work primarily with faculty and researchers, and will...

Plan and carry out programs and services of:

- Collection development and preservation
- In-depth reference and research assistance
- Classroom instruction assistance and participation
- Original cataloging

{

Provide support services to the
Services Group and the Resources
Group, including:

Support Group will include a few professional staff members and many technical and support staff members, and
will . . .

- Acquisition of library materials
- Production of bibliographic records
- Processing of library materials
- Photographic services
- Routine computer services
- Facilities management and security
- Fiscal control

More detailed descriptions of these major units and their subordinate units are presented in the following sections of this chapter.
Staffing plans for each are presented in Chapter III. These units
and the way in which major functions should be distributed among
them are shown in Exhibit 22.

The Services Group

Reader services encompass a range of library programs and services.
In the present plan of organization, highly skilled professionals
are assigned to many positions involving direct contact with library
users, regardless of the sophistication of the encounter. These same
professionals also have additional responsibilities such as book selection, program planning, current awareness, development of bibliographies, in-depth reference, and maintenance of faculty relations.

In evaluating the present plan of organization, it was found valuable to categorize library programs presently offered as a basis
for organizing and staffing these services according to skill requirements and user needs. Three categories of reader services have
been defined:

- Primary, first-line services to help library users understand
  and utilize the immediate facility and available information
  resources
- Intermediate, second-line services to interpret library resources
  in terms of specific, individual information requests
- Advanced, third-line services to relate the library information
  resources to serve the advanced scholarly and research needs
  of the academic community

EXHIBIT 22
COLUMBIA UNIVERSITY
RECOMMENDED OVERALL PLAN OF ORGANIZATION
— MAJOR UNITS AND FUNCTIONS

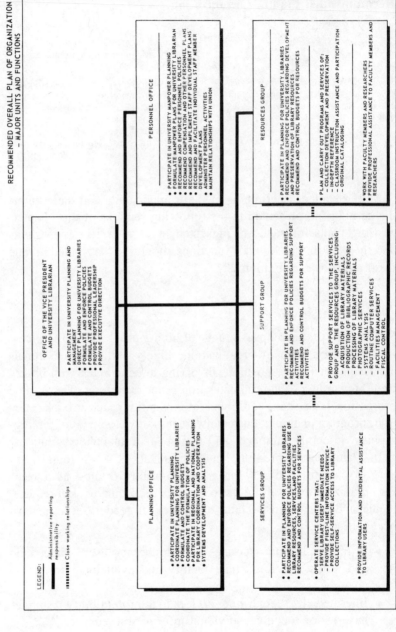

LEGEND:
———— Administrative reporting
responsibility
••••••• Close working relationships

OFFICE OF THE VICE PRESIDENT
AND UNIVERSITY LIBRARIAN

• PARTICIPATE IN UNIVERSITY PLANNING AND
  MANAGEMENT
• DIRECT PLANNING FOR UNIVERSITY LIBRARIES
• FORMULATE AND ENFORCE PERSONNEL POLICIES
• FORMULATE AND CONTROL BUDGETS
• PROVIDE PROFESSIONAL LEADERSHIP
• PROVIDE EXECUTIVE DIRECTION

PERSONNEL OFFICE

• PARTICIPATE IN UNIVERSITY MANPOWER PLANNING
• FORMULATE MANPOWER PLANS FOR UNIVERSITY LIBRARIAN
• RECOMMEND AND ENFORCE PERSONNEL POLICIES
• RECOMMEND COMPENSATION AND OTHER PERSONNEL PLANS
• RECOMMEND AND IMPLEMENT STAFF DEVELOPMENT PLANS
• RECOMMEND AND FACILITATE INDIVIDUAL STAFF MEMBER
  DEVELOPMENT PLANS
• ADMINISTER PERSONNEL ACTIVITIES
• MAINTAIN RELATIONSHIPS WITH UNION

RESOURCES GROUP

• PARTICIPATE IN PLANNING FOR UNIVERSITY LIBRARIES
• RECOMMEND AND ENFORCE POLICIES REGARDING DEVELOPMENT
  AND PRESERVATION OF LIBRARY RESOURCES
• RECOMMEND AND CONTROL BUDGETS FOR RESOURCES

• PLAN AND CARRY OUT PROGRAMS AND SERVICES OF:
  — COLLECTION DEVELOPMENT AND PRESERVATION
  — IN-DEPTH REFERENCE
  — CLASSROOM INSTRUCTION ASSISTANCE AND PARTICIPATION
  — ORIGINAL CATALOGING

• WORK WITH FACULTY MEMBERS AND RESEARCHERS
• PROVIDE PROFESSIONAL ASSISTANCE TO FACULTY MEMBERS AND
  RESEARCHERS

PLANNING OFFICE

• PARTICIPATE IN UNIVERSITY PLANNING
• COORDINATE PLANNING FOR UNIVERSITY LIBRARIES
• FORMULATE AND CONTROL BUDGETS
• COORDINATE THE FORMULATION OF POLICIES
• PARTICIPATE IN REGIONAL AND NATIONAL PLANNING
  FOR LIBRARY COORDINATION AND COOPERATION
• SYSTEMS DEVELOPMENT AND ANALYSIS

SUPPORT GROUP

• PARTICIPATE IN PLANNING FOR UNIVERSITY LIBRARIES
• RECOMMEND AND ENFORCE POLICIES REGARDING SUPPORT
  ACTIVITIES
• RECOMMEND AND CONTROL BUDGETS FOR SUPPORT
  ACTIVITIES

• PROVIDE SUPPORT SERVICES TO THE SERVICES
  GROUP AND THE RESOURCES GROUP, INCLUDING:
  — ACQUISITION OF LIBRARY MATERIALS
  — PRODUCTION OF BIBLIOGRAPHIC RECORDS
  — PROCESSING OF LIBRARY MATERIALS
  — PHOTOGRAPHIC SERVICES
  — SYSTEMS ANALYSIS
  — ROUTINE COMPUTER SERVICES
  — FACILITIES MANAGEMENT
  — FISCAL CONTROL

SERVICES GROUP

• PARTICIPATE IN PLANNING FOR UNIVERSITY LIBRARIES
• RECOMMEND AND ENFORCE POLICIES REGARDING USE OF
  LIBRARY RESOURCES, SERVICES, AND FACILITIES
• RECOMMEND AND CONTROL BUDGETS FOR SERVICES

• OPERATE SERVICE CENTERS THAT:
  — SERVE LIBRARY USERS' IMMEDIATE NEEDS
  — PROVIDE FIRST-LINE INFORMATION SERVICES
  — PROVIDE SELF-SERVICE ACCESS TO LIBRARY
    COLLECTIONS

• PROVIDE INFORMATION AND INCIDENTAL ASSISTANCE
  TO LIBRARY USERS

In considering the demands of primary and intermediate services, it was apparent that, while some professional leadership was indeed required at strategic points, many of the activities could be as well carried out by well-trained staff members who are not professional librarians. To be effective, those delivering first- and second-line services would need to be knowledgeable about library resources and their access points and be able to orient and direct users properly to the service needed. These activities would not, however, require the extensive academic training and competence of a professional librarian. The professional role would be to design, plan, oversee, and evaluate the service mechanisms needed and to develop competent staff resources to serve the user directly.

In accordance with this analysis, the proposed plan of organization of Columbia's libraries provides for the establishment of a Services Group. The group, headed by an Associate University Librarian, should be responsible for providing library services to members of the academic community on a day-to-day basis. It should be responsible for a spectrum of direct and basic service delivery and associated support systems, including the operation of subject centers, first- and second-line information services, self-service access to library collections, and maintenance of facilities. Specifically, these include:

- Primary, first-line services to help library users understand and utilize the immediate facility and available information resources

  —Explanation of library rules, regulations, and procedures
  —Directory assistance in identifying the location of required facilities, services, or materials
  —Reader assistance in general organization and use of catalog
  —Circulation of library materials
  —Borrowing required materials not in present collection
  —Providing photocopy services to duplicate materials
  —Paging requested materials
  —Support activities of reshelving, shifting, cleaning, repairing, and maintaining collections
  —Operation of self-service units such as reading and study facilities
  —Collection security

- Intermediate, second-line services to interpret resources in terms of specific, individual information requirements

  —Identification of required materials through use of bibliographies, indexes, abstracts, or other bibliographic tools
  —Determination of materials available locally through the use of holding lists, catalogs, or other tools
  —Interpretation of library files and records
  —Location of required materials not available locally
  —Instruction in the use of library tools, resources, and services
  —Assistance in determining answers to requests for facts, data, addresses, or other information problems of a general nature

In addition to these specific activities, the Services Group should have overall responsibility for (1) participation in planning for the university libraries, particularly in regard to the development of service capabilities; (2) development and enforcement of policies regarding use of library collections, services, and facilities; and (3) recommendation and control of budgets for units and staff in the services area.

The Services Group should comprise three major organizational units or subject centers: a Humanistic and Historical Studies Center, a Social Science Center, and a Science Information Center. Initially, the available facilities will not permit complete geographic consolidation of all operating units into these three centers. Furthermore, the scope of the study did not permit the consultants to reach a professional conviction that physical consolidation would be desirable in all cases.

Each of the subject centers within the Services Group should be organized internally to include:

- An *Access Services Department* to provide direct assistance in locating required library materials locally or elsewhere and to administer large-scale circulation services and operation and maintenance of facilities that expedite access to and use of the collections. Specific areas of responsibility include:

  —Catalog assistance
  —Bibliographic assistance
  —Directional information
  —Supervision of circulation and stack operations

—Operation of interlibrary loan and servicing of microforms
—Periodical and document reading rooms

- An *Instructional Materials and Services Department* to provide assistance to undergraduates, graduates, and users new to the library system in understanding and effectively using library resources and services. This activity should be a priority concern of each center and include the provision of student advisory services, reserve book services, and duplicate collections services.
- *Allied libraries* to provide geographically decentralized services. These libraries should be strongly related by subject to the primary centers and should be organized to provide a full range of services with minimal staff, relying on the subject center for leadership and support. They should not duplicate the resources of the centers and, in most cases, will represent small special collections such as the Music Library or the Fine Arts Library. The Business and Economics Library is an exception; its size and importance suggest development along a subject center line, but within the context of an allied library to the Social Science Center. (See staffing tables in Chapter III for the detailed organization and staffing of the Business and Economics Library.)

The Associate University Librarian for Services should be responsible for the development and operations of all subject centers. Directors of the subject centers should report to this officer and should be responsible for all units within their respective centers.

Allied libraries represent a more complex situation. In the small units designated as allied libraries, the senior librarian must continue to perform multiple service and resource roles. He should report to his subject center director in areas of service and facility operation, and to the appropriate department in the Resources Group in the areas of collection development and cataloging.

Exhibits 23, 24, and 25 indicate the specific departments, libraries, and other units that should be included in the three major service centers. Chapter III indicates the staff that should be assigned to the units.

OFFICE OF THE VICE PRESIDENT AND UNIVERSITY LIBRARIAN

SERVICES GROUP
Associate University Librarian

SOCIAL SCIENCE CENTER (AT LEHMAN) Director
(EXHIBIT 24)

HUMANISTIC AND HISTORICAL STUDIES CENTER (AT BUTLER) Director

SCIENCE INFORMATION CENTER (AT SEELEY MUDD) Director
(EXHIBIT 25)

INSTRUCTIONAL MATERIALS AND SERVICES DEPARTMENT Head

DUPLICATE COLLECTIONS LIBRARY Attendant

RESERVE SERVICES READING ROOM Attendant

STUDENT ADVISORY UNIT Librarian

ACCESS SERVICES DEPARTMENT Head

MICROFORM READING ROOM Attendant

DOCUMENTS ROOM Attendant

PERIODICAL READING ROOM Attendant

CIRCULATION UNIT Specialist

STACK OPERATION SECTION Supervisor

PATERNO LIBRARY Attendant

INFORMATION AND CATALOG ASSISTANCE UNIT Librarian

INTERLIBRARY LOAN SERVICES UNIT Librarian

SUPPORT AND SEARCHING SECTION Supervisor

ALLIED LIBRARIES

FINE ARTS LIBRARY Librarian

MUSIC LIBRARY Librarian

LIBRARY SERVICE LIBRARY Librarian

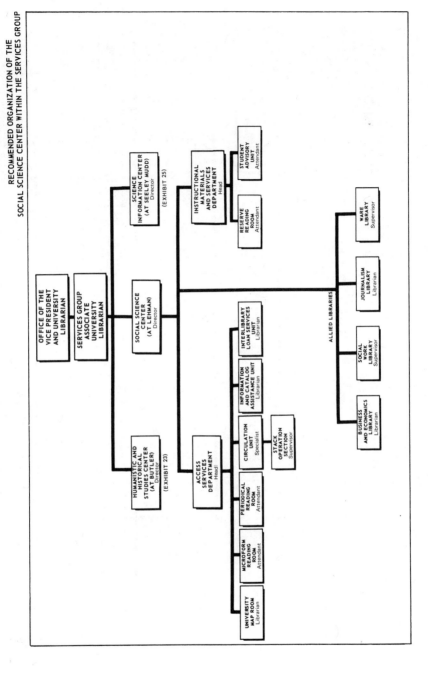

EXHIBIT 25

COLUMBIA UNIVERSITY

RECOMMENDED ORGANIZATION OF THE
SCIENCE INFORMATION CENTER WITHIN THE SERVICES GROUP

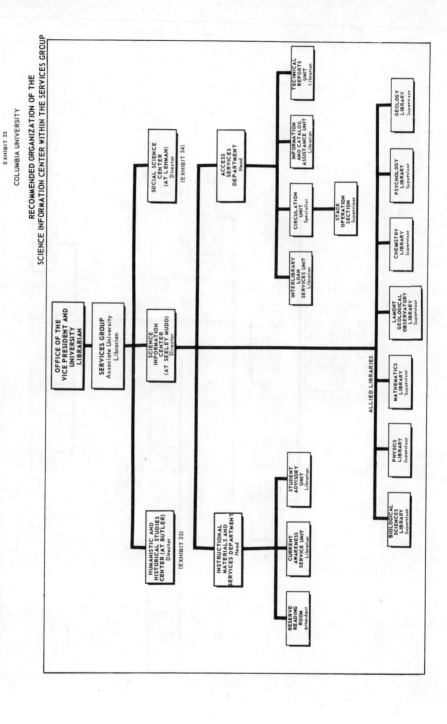

The Resources Group

The Resources Group should bring together subject-oriented professional librarian skills and direct them toward the development, organization, preservation, and utilization of the information resources required by the academic community. Individuals in the group should be given the flexibility to perform without the burden of desk schedules and less complex information requests. In addition to meeting rigorous and demanding library service requests, this group should provide dynamic library services that go beyond the boundaries of the library and into the classroom, the professor's office, and the scholarly meeting. The basic functions of the Resources Group should be to build library collections, make available a wide array of sophisticated subject and technical capabilities, and draw upon external resources effectively. An integral part of this responsibility will be to provide advanced, third-line reader services that serve the sophisticated information needs of the academic community. These activities include:

- Advising and counseling faculty and students to capitalize on library resources and services in dealing with specific instructional and research problems, such as the strategy for a thesis
- Providing detailed, in-depth reference assistance by subject-competent specialists
- Relating library resources to instructional programs by working in planning projects, developing curricula, making presentations in classrooms, and making the library a teaching laboratory
- Developing relations with and among reader service units aimed at coordinating programs, collections, and services; monitoring the flow of user requests and the success with which they are handled; and sharing mutually useful information on professional and organizational topics
- Securing appropriate resources by identifying new materials needed in developing collections and monitoring the acquisition policies of all units within the system
- Establishing the organization and bibliographic control of library resources, including creation of original catalog records, bibliographic policies, authority rules, points of access, and thesauri

- Identifying materials that require preservation decisions in terms of binding, microfilming, special care, reprinting, or other maintenance activities
- Planning, developing, and operating current awareness activities such as annotated lists of new acquisitions or SDI programs

  —Teaching and research in library-related subject fields
  —Planning and program development for reader services

In addition, the Resources Group should have overall responsibility for planning the resource capability of the university libraries, recommending policies regarding development and organization of resources, preparing budgets for operation of the Resources Group and for collection development, and providing professional assistance to faculty members and researchers.

The Resources Group should be headed by the Associate University Librarian for Resources. He should possess the academic credentials and presence to perform as the primary liaison with the academic community and provide intellectual and professional leadership to the resources staff.

Two major divisions within the Resources Group should focus professional activities along the functional lines of (1) development and use of resources and (2) organization and bibliographic control of materials:

- *The Resource Development and Utilization Division* should have units corresponding to each of the three subject centers and should perform required collection development activities, backup reference support, and subject-oriented faculty and research liaison. In addition, the division should coordinate the resource development capabilities in the law, medical, and distinctive collections libraries.
- *The Bibliographic Control Division* should have units for the subject centers and the law, medical, and distinctive collections libraries. This division should exercise administrative control over the cataloging activities in all areas of the library system. Cataloging responsibilities should cover both monographs and serials.

In addition to the major divisions, the Resources Group, under the direction of the Associate University Librarian for Resources, should establish two staff assistant positions.

- The *Coordinator of Instructional Programs* should be responsible for coordinating instructional programs of the libraries in terms of working with committees, developing new programs, and operating a lecture schedule.
- The *Coordinator of Current Awareness Programs* should be responsible for coordinating the current awareness activities in terms of identifying unmet requirements, planning programs, and developing special operations such as use of census tapes.

It is recognized that the same staff may have the subject or technical competence to function in both of the above divisions, performing cataloging, selection, preservation, and in-depth research and reference activities. These staff members will need to maintain multiple reporting relationships and their respective supervisors will need to negotiate the allocation of time among the different units and activities, with appropriate input from the individual.

The staff should comprise primarily highly qualified librarians, many of whom should have multiple qualifications. The staffing complement of the group should work closely with faculty members, as proposed earlier in this chapter.

In some respects, the proposal to establish a Resources Group parallels twentieth century university practice in Germany where, under the *Referatsystem*, highly qualified individuals (*Referenten*) provide specialized materials selection, collection building, and reference services.

Exhibit 26 indicates the specific divisions, departments, and offices that should be included in the Resources Group.

The Support Group

A Support Group should be established to provide essential business, analysis, and record production services for all of Columbia's libraries. The Support Group brings together an array of technical, highly specialized support skills into a tightly organized environment aimed at providing highly efficient services. Performance measure-

EXHIBIT 26

COLUMBIA UNIVERSITY

RECOMMENDED ORGANIZATION
OF THE RESOURCES GROUP

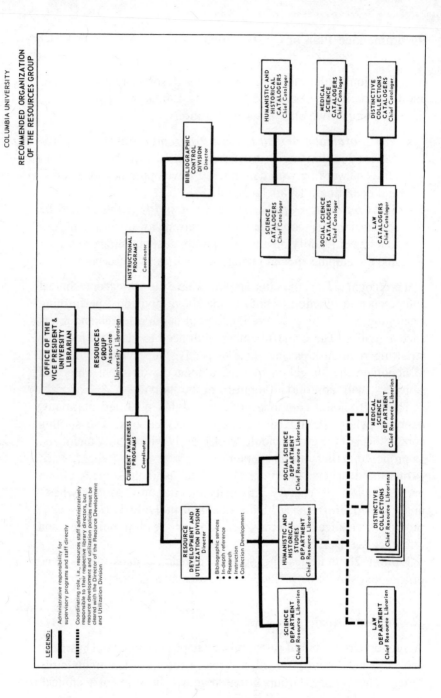

LEGEND:

▬▬▬ Administrative responsibility for
supervisory programs and staff directly

▪▪▪▪▪▪ Coordinating role, i.e., resources staff administratively
responsible to their respective library directors, but
resource development and utilization policies must be
cleared with the Director of the Resource Development
and Utilization Division

OFFICE OF THE
VICE PRESIDENT &
UNIVERSITY
LIBRARIAN

RESOURCES
GROUP
Associate
University Librarian

INSTRUCTIONAL
PROGRAMS
Coordinator

CURRENT AWARENESS
PROGRAMS
Coordinator

BIBLIOGRAPHIC
CONTROL
DIVISION
Director

HUMANISTIC AND
HISTORICAL
CATALOGERS
Chief Cataloger

SCIENCE
CATALOGERS
Chief Cataloger

MEDICAL
SCIENCE
CATALOGERS
Chief Cataloger

SOCIAL SCIENCE
CATALOGERS
Chief Cataloger

DISTINCTIVE
COLLECTIONS
CATALOGERS
Chief Cataloger

LAW
CATALOGERS
Chief Cataloger

RESOURCE
DEVELOPMENT AND
UTILIZATION DIVISION
Director

• Bibliographic services
• In-depth reference
• Research
• Instruction
• Collection Development

SCIENCE
DEPARTMENT
Chief Resource Librarian

HUMANISTIC AND
HISTORICAL
STUDIES
DEPARTMENT
Chief Resource Librarian

SOCIAL SCIENCE
DEPARTMENT
Chief Resource Librarian

LAW
DEPARTMENT
Chief Resource Librarian

DISTINCTIVE
COLLECTIONS
Chief Resource Librarians

MEDICAL
SCIENCE
DEPARTMENT
Chief Resource Librarian

ments, both qualitative and quantitative, should be emphasized, and nonlibrarian capabilities should be utilized extensively. The basic functions of the Support Group should be to administer:

- Acquisition of materials
- Production of bibliographic access records
- Preparation of library materials for use in service units
- Facilities management and security
- Fiscal control and financial reports
- Preservation services
- Photographic services
- Routine computer services

In addition, the Support Group should have overall responsibility for planning in its area, developing support activity policies, and recommending budgets.

The Support Group should be headed by the Associate University Librarian for Support who should act largely as a coordinator of the diverse activities of the group. It should not be expected that he have technical expertise in each activity, but he should be able to evaluate, understand, and manage plans and programs in these several areas.

The Support Group, as shown in Exhibit 27, should comprise two major departments: the Records and Materials Processing Department, and the Business Services Department.

- The *Records and Materials Processing Department* should be responsible for the acquisition and processing of library materials into the system, and for producing bibliographic records, including cataloging with available copy. The department should be organized with two sections based on activity performed and three sections based on form of material, as shown in Exhibit 28.

  —The *Bibliographic Searching Unit* should perform all types of searching—acquisition, cataloging, foreign language—for all types of materials: monographs, serials, documents, and reports. This unit should act as the switching point to direct incoming orders to their proper processing unit. It should offer the distinct advantages of organization around skills

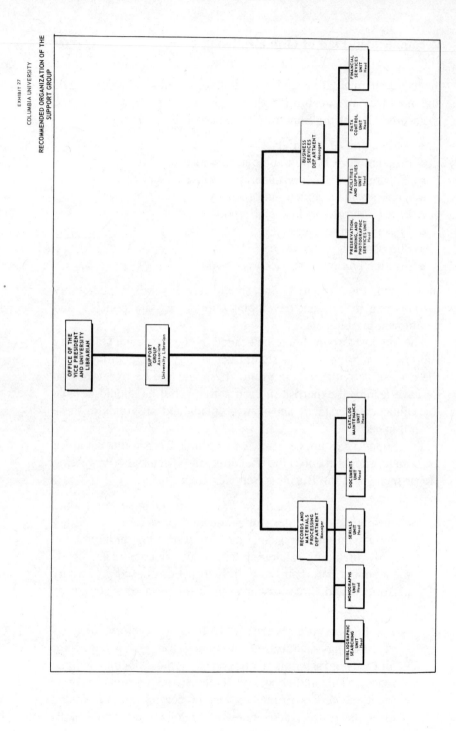

EXHIBIT 28

COLUMBIA UNIVERSITY

RECOMMENDED ORGANIZATION
OF THE RECORDS AND MATERIALS PROCESSING
DEPARTMENT WITHIN THE SUPPORT GROUP

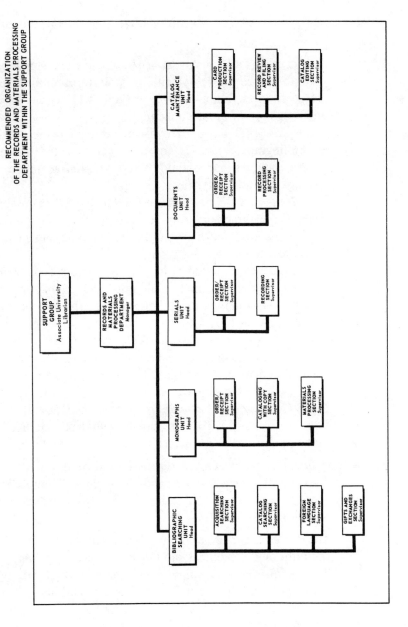

and access to tools. It should also facilitate a one-stop biblio-graphic search, development of a uniform bibliographic record form to follow the life of the newly acquired item, and reduction of order duplication.

—The *Catalog Maintenance Unit* should receive and monitor all bibliographic records for consistency with Columbia catalog policies and should file, edit, and maintain the catalogs and authority files.

—The *Monographs Unit* should be responsible for the complete cycle of monograph ordering, receiving, processing, prepara-tion of records, and distribution of materials and records. Three subsections are suggested.

—The *Serials Unit* should order, receive, and record serials. It should not do original cataloging, and major emphasis should be on updating central holdings records and processing of materials for binding.

—The *Documents Unit* should order, receive, and distribute documents. It is suggested that cataloging government reports and other documents be replaced with the utilization of avail-able bibliographic systems such as the *Monthly Catalog of U. S. Government Publications.* Documents that are excep-tions and require special treatment should be cataloged as monographs by the Resources Group.

• The *Business Services Department* should be responsible for the several auxiliary services and the technical preservation support required by the libraries. Four units are suggested, as shown in Exhibit 29.

—The *Preservation, Binding, and Photographic Services Unit* should provide technical support in the indicated areas.

—The *Facilities and Supplies Unit* should work closely with University Buildings and Grounds, and should order, main-tain, and dispense required library supplies.

—The *Financial Services Unit* should maintain accounts and produce financial reports.

—The *Data Control Unit* should operate the various routine automated systems and provide programming support.

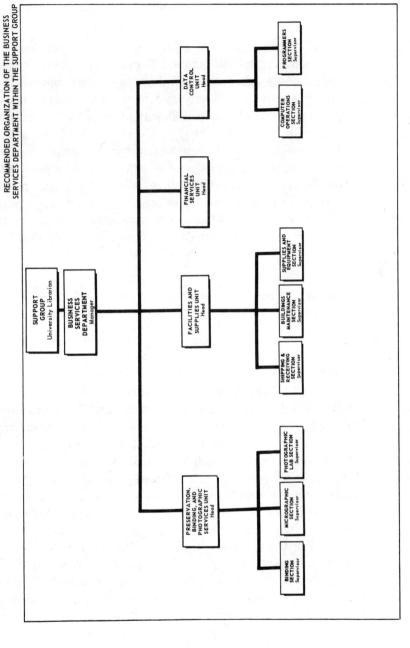

Serious consideration was also given to adding responsibilities for operations research and automated systems design to this Support Group. Locating such functions in this key library unit could well be appropriate in some library systems on the grounds that such important activities are compatible with those of the Support Group and represent important central services that should be available to all other units. However, upon further study compelling arguments were made for placing operations research and systems development in the Planning Office. This office will need to utilize all the technology it can in its planning efforts and is in a strategic position close to library leadership that can be responsive to priority problem areas where new systems might be needed or operations research techniques applied.

Distinctive Collections, Law Library Center, and
Medical Science Information Center

The recommended plan of organization also provides for a few very unusual library units to be responsible directly to the Vice President and University Librarian. These units, due to historic factors or to collection strength or distinctiveness, need to be kept administratively separate from the Services and Resources Groups. There are several reasons for this separation. Certain distinctive collections serve not only Columbia, but also—because of their uniqueness and depth—scholars from all over the world, and need to be administered somewhat differently. In the case of rare and primary source materials, preservation problems and access policies are different from those in the subject centers. Users of these collections also tend to be experienced in their library requirements so that fewer first- and second-line services are needed compared with subject-competent, in-depth reference, and other professional resource capabilities. Thus, the full range of activities provided in these library components needs to be administratively consolidated rather than separated into specialized resource and service components.

Funding patterns also differ for distinctive collections, since they depend more on gifts and income from patrons than on general university support. Some degree of separation enhances the status of these collections and anticipates the possibility of their being ultimately recognized formally and supported as a truly national resource.

The Law Library Center and the Medical Science Information Center should continue to report directly to the University Librarian. Because of the largely technical and specialized nature and use of their collections, these libraries do not lend themselves to incorporation within the services and resources groups as is desirable for most of the system's libraries.

It should be stressed that in all respects, however, these libraries are integral components of the total library system. The significance of this special arrangement is in the nature of the relationship of these libraries with the resources and services groups, not that they are any less fully parts of the whole system. Aggressive efforts should be made to coordinate all facets of the total system, including these special units. Collection development officers, resource librarians, and reference librarians of these units should have formal coordinating, advisory, and communications roles with the Resource Development and Utilization Division.

The directors of these units should also be involved directly and continually in the decision making, policy making, and planning groups of the library system. These professionals possess outstanding capabilities that can be utilized in areas other than their specialty.

The unique units defined in the Columbia context are:

- Law Library Center
- Medical Science Information Center
- University Archival Collections
- Manuscripts and Rare Books Collections
- Architecture Collections
- East Asian Collections

In Exhibit 30, following this page, a plan of internal organization for the Law Library Center is shown. A parallel plan for the Medical Science Information Center is included as Exhibit 31. The distinctive collections, having very small staffs, do not require formal internal plans of organization.

Staffing of each of the centers and collections is proposed in Chapter III.

EXHIBIT 30

COLUMBIA UNIVERSITY

RECOMMENDED ORGANIZATION OF THE
LAW LIBRARY CENTER

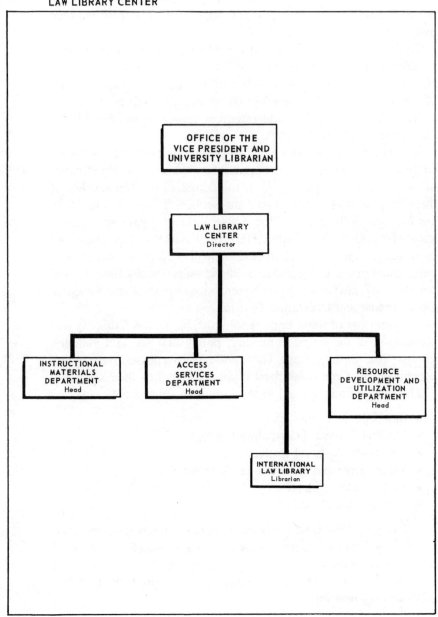

EXHIBIT 31

COLUMBIA UNIVERSITY

RECOMMENDED ORGANIZATION OF THE MEDICAL
SCIENCE INFORMATION CENTER

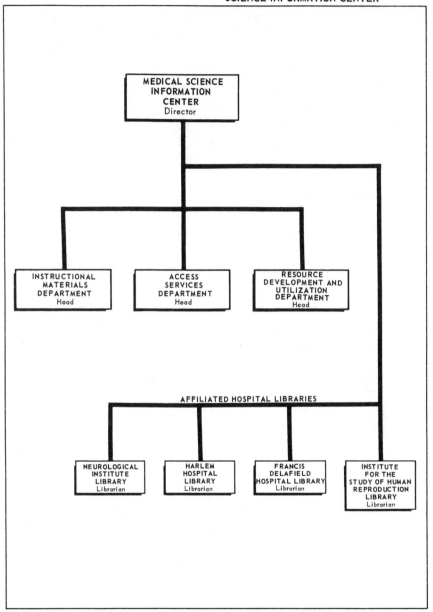

The Personnel Office

The human resources of the libraries are so important that the highest level of attention should be given to the personnel function. The Personnel Office, headed by an Assistant University Librarian, should operate as an integral part of the top management of Columbia's libraries. The specific responsibilities of the Personnel Office of Columbia's libraries should be to:

- Participate in university manpower planning
- Formulate manpower plans for the university libraries and submit them to the Vice President and University Librarian for approval
- Recommend and implement personnel policies within the libraries
- Recommend compensation and other personnel plans for the libraries
- Recommend and implement staff development plans for the libraries' executive, librarian, specialist, and clerical staff
- Recommend and facilitate individual staff members' development plans
- Administer personnel activities
- Maintain relationships with the union

The Assistant University Librarian for Personnel should work directly with the Vice President and University Librarian. He should provide staff assistance to and serve as secretary of the important Staff Development Committee.

The Planning Office

Comprehensive planning is a top management function to which the Vice President and University Librarian should give continuing personal attention and leadership. A Planning Office, headed by an Assistant University Librarian, should assist him in this. The responsibilities assigned to the Planning Office and the Assistant University Librarian for Planning should be to:

- Participate in university planning as the representative of the Vice President and University Librarian

- Coordinate planning for the university libraries by:
  —Developing and maintaining basic series of data required for planning
  —Preparing planning guides and schedules for use by all library units
  —Counseling and assisting library unit heads engaged in planning
  —Integrating plans formulated by library units
- Formulate and control budgets by:
  —Coordinating the preparation of budget requests in accordance with university directives and guidelines
  —Providing library plans and guidelines needed to prepare budget requests
  —Integrating budget requests formulated by units
  —Advising and assisting the Vice President and University Librarian in preparing and submitting budget requests for the libraries
  —Reviewing budget progress and advising the Vice President and University Librarian on budget performance
- Coordinate the formulation of policies and maintenance of policy manuals
- Participate in regional and national planning for library co-ordination and cooperation
- Formulate reports and applications for grants and contracts for funding agencies

In addition, the Planning Office should be responsible for overseeing library research and analysis. Specifically it should be responsible for applying (1) computer and automation technology to the library system and (2) specialized management expertise to library problems. These activities have intrinsic importance for effective planning. Moreover, as costly developmental expenditures can be involved it is important that these activities be placed close to top library leadership. The addition of these functions can be time consuming and distract the energies of the Planning Office unless adequate safeguards are made. Thus, the library should be prepared to add a staff position in the Planning Office to manage these functions in order that the Planning Officer's attention to the ongoing problems of planning can be assured.

The Planning Office will require a small staff. Hence, no internal chart of organization is required.

THE TOP MANAGEMENT TEAM

The Vice President and University Librarian should provide executive direction and professional leadership to Columbia's libraries. The heads of the five major units should work closely with him on a "professional partnership" basis as the libraries' top management team. These key executives should share the same library philosophies and objectives. Confidence and communication among them should be extremely high. They should share a feeling of total responsibility for the effectiveness and the problems of Columbia libraries.

The top management team should meet as a group at least weekly. There should be daily communication between the Vice President and University Librarian and each of the other five top executives. Each of the five should have easy access to him. There should be frequent communication—at least two or three times a week—between and among each of the five top executives.

CLOSE WORKING RELATIONSHIPS

A research library must operate as a unified whole in conducting its total work even though it needs to be organized in manageable units to carry on activities on a day-to-day basis. It should therefore be recognized that under the recommended plan of overall organization, the six major units, including the Office of the Vice President and University Librarian, are mutually interdependent and should work together closely and cooperatively.

Exhibit 32 shows graphically the mutual interdependence of the six major units. It indicates that:

- There is a substantial interdependence of the Office of the

EXHIBIT 32

COLUMBIA UNIVERSITY

RECOMMENDED RELATIONSHIPS
AMONG MAJOR UNITS

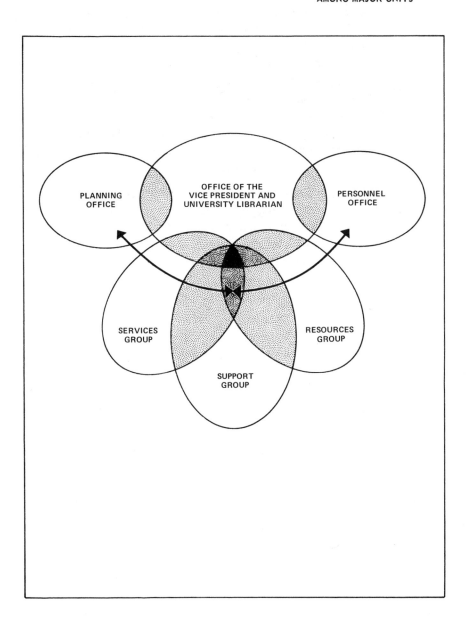

Vice President and University Librarian and each of the other
five units individually as well as between the Office of the
Vice President and two or more of the other units at the same
time
- There is substantial interdependence among the three major
operating groups: the Services Group, the Resources Group,
and the Support Group.
- The two principal staff offices—the Planning Office and the
Personnel Office—are, in effect, part of the Office of the
Vice President and University Librarian. They relate directly
to each other and to the three groups.

Close working relationships should be developed, as proposed
in Chapter IV, in planning, policy formulation, budget formulation,
working communication, and staff development.

Chapter III, which follows, presents recommendations on how
the plan of organization should be staffed. Chapter IV then
suggests approaches for making the plan of organization effective in carrying out management and professional activities.

Recommended Plan
of Staffing

The ability of Columbia's libraries to meet the requirements of the future will be determined by the quality, utilization, and productivity of the staff and the manner in which the staff is organized. It will depend in part on designing positions that capitalize fully on individual capabilities, training, and talents, and in part on giving staff clear and meaningful assignments in the organization. Assignments should be geared to performing the services, resources, and support functions of the libraries well and designed to foster career and personal development opportunities throughout the system.

The recommended plan of staffing presented in this chapter is designed to prepare Columbia's libraries to meet these challenges and to perform effectively within the organization plan described in Chapter II. The staffing plan recommended involves substantial change from present patterns at Columbia and represents, perhaps, a fundamental departure from traditional plans commonly found at other research libraries. Implementation of these changes will require considerable immediate reorientation of staff, particularly professional staff members, to new roles and responsibilities. It will also depend heavily on the libraries' developing ongoing training programs in management approaches and techniques to prepare managerial and supervisory staff to perform effectively within the complex library system. Finally, implementation of the recommended plan will require well-designed staff development and personnel plans that are described in Chapter IV.

Implementation of the staffing plan thus represents no less of a challenge than does adaptation to the proposed plan of organization. The combined effect of carrying out these recommendations at Columbia, however, should be to improve the libraries' capabilities to develop and perform at a high level of proficiency while offering a previously unavailable level of sophisticated support to the academic community.

REQUIREMENTS OF THE FUTURE

Columbia's libraries have highly qualified professional staff and support personnel. The libraries have benefited from a tradition of strong executive and professional library leadership and from active support from the university's top administration. The plan of staffing should build on these strengths to enhance the development of staff capabilities that will be needed to meet changing library resource and service requirements of the university.

Trends in Higher Education

Staffing should be geared to meet the future requirements of higher education generally and at Columbia in particular. Research libraries will need to define and develop more varied and sophisticated collection and staff capabilities. The academic community will more and more depend upon the subject-competent librarian to interpret and provide efficient access to the complex collections. Faculty and students will need, in effect, professionals who are sensitive to their needs and able to help them filter out from the vast proliferation of published material in every discipline those resources most relevant to their instructional and research interests. Individualized study will bring the librarian more often into contact with students who have special needs for instructional assistance. These and other trends portend the growing opportunity and obligation which research libraries have to develop professional and other staff capabilities that can offer an array of needed services to the undergraduate user as well as to the sophisticated faculty member and research scholar.

Present staffing plans at Columbia do not adequately equip the libraries to meet these challenges. The expanding resources and changing emphases of the structures to sustain high levels of professional performance and growth while accommodating to the sheer volume of day-to-day operating demands. Many so-called professional positions mix routine clerical duties with professional responsibilities so that the librarian's role has become blurred. As a result, despite the increasingly sophisticated and specialized requirements of library users, the individual staff member's ability to focus on matters important to the user and to his own development has been impaired.

The plan of staffing recommended is designed specifically to overcome these limitations at Columbia.

Principles of Staffing

Evaluation of present staffing patterns at Columbia in terms of principles developed through experience in a variety of institutions that can be applied to research libraries indicates several limitations which should be overcome. Of particular importance to Columbia's ability to cope effectively with future requirements is the inadequacy of present staffing patterns in focusing professional effort and in developing specialized capabilities and career opportunities. Because advancement tends to follow administrative lines, librarians interested in careers in a subject area or professional field are limited in their opportunities for career progression. The present plan tends to force excellent staff into administrative positions as the only channel for advancement in the system. In addition, professionals with responsibility for particular small operating units often perform nonprofessional and clerical tasks to justify their full-time assignment to the position; this, of course, diminishes user access to and utilization of these highly skilled librarians.

The recommended staffing plan is designed to enable the Columbia libraries to overcome these limitations and to conform more closely to sound staffing principles.

A NEW COMPREHENSIVE PLAN

OF STAFFING

Columbia University should adopt a comprehensive plan of staffing for its libraries. The plan should comprise two major elements:

- A plan for structuring positions
- A plan for assigning specific numbers of positions to organization units

The staffing plan should be matched to the recommended plan of organization for Columbia's libraries set forth in Chapter II. Once the plan is adopted, individuals should be selected and developed to fill positions, following the approaches to staff development outlined in Chapter IV. The plan itself should be kept up to date through the approach to manpower planning also recommended in Chapter IV.

A proposed comprehensive plan of library staffing is set forth in this chapter. The plan gives particular attention to identifying new professional and specialist positions needed to develop capabilities in each of the functional areas:

- *Services*—Providing first- and second-line access and information as well as instructional assistance to users of the various library collections and facilities at Columbia
- *Resources*—Providing subject knowledge on collection development, bibliographic control, in-depth reference, and sophisticated research and instructional assistance.
- *Support*—Providing technical and business support for the processing of materials and administration required to accomplish the service and resource objectives of the libraries
- *Administrative Management*—Providing overall executive leadership and staff support to the conduct and development of library programs and resources, including personnel and planning activities

The recommended plan classifies positions according to their importance within the library system, recognizing the need for a hierarchy of skills, subject and technical competence, responsibility, and authority. The plan has been designed to yield several important benefits—specifically, to:

- Establish positions that involve exclusively or primarily professional pursuits
- Provide parallel opportunities for professional advancement for those interested in the areas of services, resources, and management, respectively
- Heighten staff performance by redefining the scope of professional and other positions to facilitate greater sophistication and depth of focus in specialized areas
- Enhance job fulfillment for all staff while at the same time improving library capabilities

Implementation of the recommended plan will require substantial reorientation of staff to new roles, responsibilities, and reporting relationships. It should not, however, require a significant net addition of people, although filling newly defined positions may result in some personnel shifts and turnover.

Costs of implementing the recommended plan will depend less on the proposed structure than on the compensation plans adopted by Columbia. The plans adopted should be compatible with the classification scheme recommended in this chapter. This will probably result in some realignment of salaries owing to the lack of a sound classification and compensation system at Columbia. As the compensation plan is developed, salaries will have to be set for new positions (especially specialist positions) for which market information and experience will need to be obtained before the full cost impact will be known.

A PLAN FOR STRUCTURING POSITIONS
TO MEET WORK REQUIREMENTS

A new plan for structuring staff positions should be adopted for use at Columbia's libraries. The plan should define positions, taking into account the specific work requirements and activities to be performed, and classify them into meaningful categories.

The plan of organization set forth in Chapter II calls for the libraries to be organized quite differently from before, especially with respect to the Services, Support, and Resources Groups. As explained in Chapter II, the work to be performed by these three

EXHIBIT 33

COLUMBIA UNIVERSITY

CATEGORIES OF POSITIONS THAT SHOULD BE
ESTABLISHED TO MEET WORK REQUIREMENTS

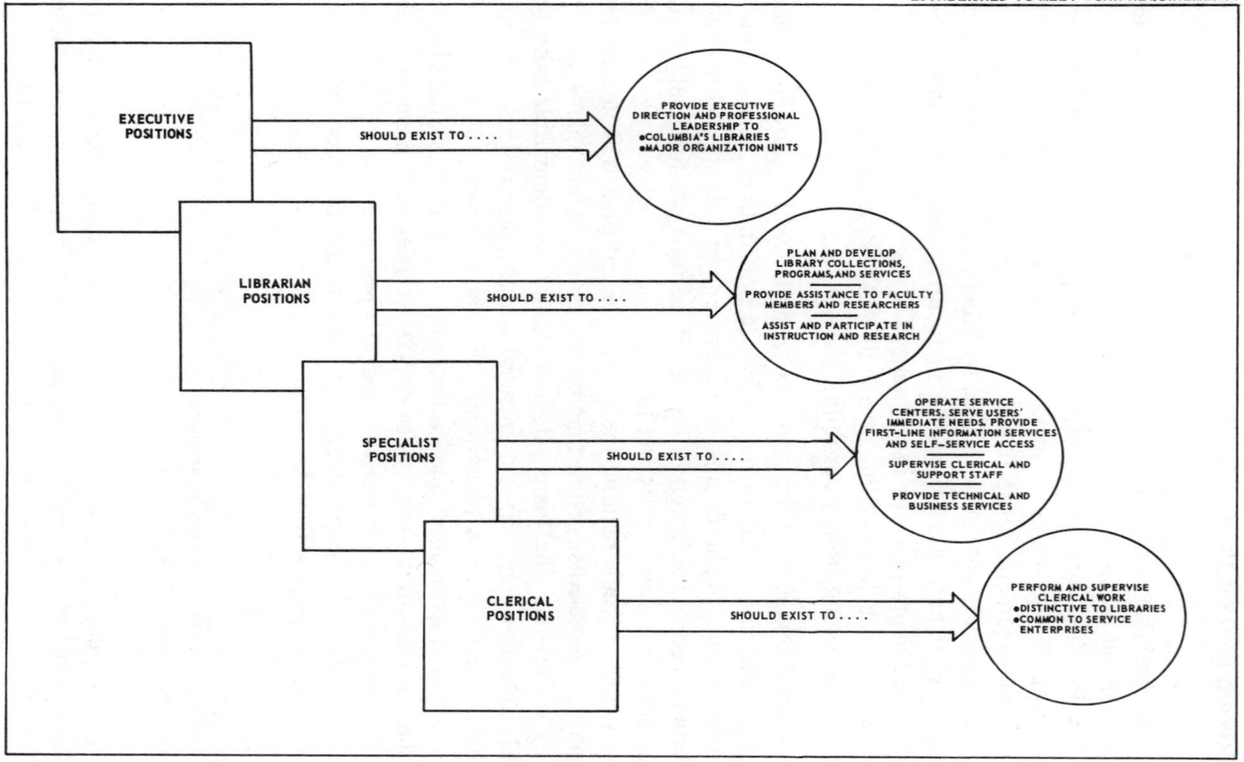

groups will require that new and different positions be established. Accordingly, the proposed plan calls for library positions to be classified into four major categories: executive, librarian, specialist, and clerical positions. Each of these categories should include the specific positions which should exist to meet specific work requirements, as indicated in Exhibit 33.

Executive Positions

Executive positions should encompass the top-management professional positions with primary professional and leadership responsibility for guiding the libraries toward achievement of objectives. For compensation purposes, five position grades should be established within the group of executive positions at Columbia's libraries. These grades should include the following recommended positions and also should allow for the addition of new positions as they may be needed in the years ahead.

- Vice President and University Librarian
- Associate University Librarian for Resources
- Associate University Librarian for Services
- Associate University Librarian for Support
- Directors of the Law Library Center and the Medical Science Information Center
- Assistant University Librarian for Personnel
- Assistant University Librarian for Planning
- Directors of Distinctive Collections
- Directors of Subject Centers
- Director of Resource Development and Utilization Division
- Director of Bibliographic Control Division

EXHIBIT 34

COLUMBIA UNIVERSITY

**RECOMMENDED STRUCTURE OF
EXECUTIVE POSITIONS**

EXECUTIVE POSITIONS

POSITION CLASSIFICATION	
E–5	VICE PRESIDENT AND UNIVERSITY LIBRARIAN
E–4	ASSOCIATE UNIVERSITY LIBRARIAN FOR RESOURCES ASSOCIATE UNIVERSITY LIBRARIAN FOR SERVICES ASSOCIATE UNIVERSITY LIBRARIAN FOR SUPPORT DIRECTORS OF THE LAW LIBRARY CENTER AND THE MEDICAL SCIENCE INFORMATION CENTER
E–3	ASSISTANT UNIVERSITY LIBRARIAN FOR PERSONNEL ASSISTANT UNIVERSITY LIBRARIAN FOR PLANNING DIRECTORS OF DISTINCTIVE COLLECTIONS
	LIBRARIAN POSITIONS
E–2	ASSISTANT UNIVERSITY LIBRARIAN FOR PERSONNEL ASSISTANT UNIVERSITY LIBRARIAN FOR PLANNING DIRECTORS OF DISTINCTIVE COLLECTIONS DIRECTOR OF SUBJECT CENTERS DIRECTOR OF RESOURCE DEVELOPMENT AND UTILIZATION DIVISION DIRECTOR OF BIBLIOGRAPHIC CONTROL DIVISION
E–1	DIRECTOR OF RESOURCES DEVELOPMENT AND UTILIZATION DIVISION DIRECTORS OF SUBJECT CENTERS DIRECTOR OF BIBLIOGRAPHIC CONTROL DIVISION MANAGERS OF SUPPORT DEPARTMENTS (RECORDS AND MATERIALS PROCESSING AND BUSINESS SERVICES) MANAGER LIBRARY RESEARCH AND ANALYSIS UNIT

5	4	3	2	1

SALARY STEPS

- Manager of Records and Materials Processing Department
- Manager of Library Research and Analysis Unit[1]
- Manager of Business Services Department

The distribution of these positions among the five executive grades is shown in Exhibit 34. As indicated in the exhibit, for flexibility, some of the executive positions are included in two salary classifications. Exhibit 35 lists the responsibilities that should be assigned to each of the recommended executive positions.

Librarian Positions

Librarian positions should be redefined to consolidate meaningful professional tasks. There should be five classes of librarian positions at Columbia. The classes should include positions for which formal training as a librarian is typically a minimum requirement for competent performance. Other academic degrees should become increasingly common requirements towards the upper levels where sophisticated service to the academic community is involved. The librarian's formal degree training and extensive practical experience allows the individual to perform as a professional with a minimum of supervision. The position is one of fundamental importance and substantive library programs and policies would be impaired if untrained personnel were involved.

The recommended librarian positions include a hierarchy of responsibilities that provide career opportunities in professional areas of services and resources as well as in administration. Advancement should depend upon an individual's performance as measured against the distinct requirements of his position, plus overall contribution and potential in his particular area of professional interest. It should be stressed that the proposed classification scheme thus encourages growth along professional as well as managerial lines.

The plan also defines many librarian positions so that staff are less burdened by operating detail and are able to focus more precisely

---

1. This position, while not explicitly provided for in the recommended plan of organization, is listed here and referred to in subsequent sections to suggest where the study team would rank the position if it were established, for example, in the Planning Office.

EXHIBIT 35 (1)

Columbia University

RECOMMENDED EXECUTIVE POSITIONS
BY CLASSIFICATION

Position Title	Position Classification	Major Responsibilities
Vice President and University Librarian	E-5	Executive direction of overall library operations, exercising professional and managerial leadership for the development of the libraries; relates to the Executive Vice President for Academic Affairs and Provost of the university along with other top administrative officials concerning academic plans and their implications for the libraries.
Associate University Librarian for Resources	E-4	Professional leadership in planning and developing the resource capabilities of the libraries, including the development, utilization, and organization of these resources to serve the Columbia academic community. This position operates as part of the top management group.
Associate University Librarian for Services	E-4	Professional leadership in planning, developing, and operating reader services, including access services to assist users in securing required materials and instructional services to help users understand and effectively use library resources which are available through the three subject centers and associated libraries. This position operates as part of the top management group.
Associate University Librarian for Support	E-4	Administration and coordination of the critical support activities provided to the Services Group, Resources Group, Law and Medical Science Libraries, and Distinctive Collections. These activities include records and materials processing, business services, library research, and data processing support. This position operates as part of the top management team.
Directors of the Law Library Center and the Medical Science Information Center	E-4	Administration of the service and resource activities of the law and medical units, including planning, developing, and operating these specialized capabilities and relating them to the university system.
Assistant University Librarian for Personnel	E-2/3	Professional leadership in planning, developing, and operating manpower plans, personnel policies and practices, work requirements, performance standards, training activities, and other staff development programs; oversees relationships with clerical staff unions as appropriate under university union agreements. This position operates as part of the top management group.
Assistant University Librarian for Planning	E-2/3	Professional leadership in developing short- and long-term overall library plans; assists the Vice President and University Librarian in representing the libraries in university planning; assists library components in the process of effective planning; and formulates operating and capital budgets to reflect adopted plans. Also can give leadership to library provisions for application of operations research and new technology. This position operates as part of the top management group.

EXHIBIT 35 (2)

Position Title	Position Classification	Major Responsibilities
Directors of Distinctive Collections	E-2/3	Administration of the service and resource activities in respective units, including planning, developing, and operating these specialized capabilities and relating them to the university system.
Directors of Subject Centers	E-1/2	Administration of the service activities provided at the subject centers and their associated libraries, including developing and coordinating the delivery of access services and instructional services; preparing short- and long-term plans, programs, and budgets; and operating required staff training programs.
Director of Resource Development and Utilization Division	E-1/2	Administration of resource policies and programs within all subject groupings as they relate to collection development and preservation as well as in-depth reference and research assistance. A primary responsibility is the cultivation and maintenance of active professional relationships with faculty members in areas such as effective use of library resources and the role of the library in the instructional process.
Director of Bibliographic Control Division	E-1/2	Administration of resource policies and programs within all subject groupings as they relate to bibliographic standards, access points, variations from established cataloging procedures, and development of catalogs. Also oversees the professional activity of original cataloging with a major goal of involving and relating staff to other critical library programs in the resources area.
Manager of Records and Materials Processing Department	E-1	Administration of activities relating to the acquisition of required materials, production of associated records, and maintenance of these records. The emphasis of this position is on developing a productive environment drawing on the professional resources available elsewhere in the organization.
Manager of Library Research and Analysis Unit	E-1	Administration of activities involved with evaluating library performance and developing programs and systems that will improve the libraries' capability to meet objectives.
Manager of Business Services Department	E-1	Administration of central business-oriented activities, including financial services, shipping and receiving, supplies, equipment, and facilities maintenance and security.

LIBRARIAN POSITIONS

POSITION CLASSIFICATION	EXECUTIVE POSITIONS				
L—5	CHIEF RESOURCE LIBRARIAN LIBRARY INSTRUCTOR				
L—4	INSTRUCTIONAL PROGRAM COORDINATOR ARCHIVIST PRESERVATION OFFICER CURRENT AWARENESS CONSULTANT RESOURCE LIBRARIAN (SUBJECT) BIBLIOGRAPHER (FORM) CHIEF CATALOGER HEAD, ACCESS SERVICES DEPARTMENT				
L—3	RESOURCE LIBRARIAN (SUBJECT) BIBLIOGRAPHER (FORM) CHIEF CATALOGER HEAD, ACCESS SERVICES DEPARTMENT HEAD, INSTRUCTIONAL MATERIALS AND SERVICES DEPARTMENT SUPERVISING LIBRARIAN STAFF DEVELOPMENT OFFICER STAFF RELATIONS OFFICER CATALOGER (SUBJECT) CATALOGER (SERIALS) HEAD, LIBRARY RESEARCH AND ANALYSIS UNIT ACCESS LIBRARIAN		SPECIALIST POSITIONS		
L—2	HEAD, INSTRUCTIONAL MATERIALS AND SERVICES DEPARTMENT SUPERVISING LIBRARIAN STAFF DEVELOPMENT OFFICER STAFF RELATIONS OFFICER CATALOGER (SUBJECT) CATALOGER (SERIALS) HEAD, LIBRARY RESEARCH AND ANALYSIS UNIT ACCESS LIBRARIAN STUDENT ADVISOR				
L—1	HEAD, LIBRARY RESEARCH AND ANALYSIS UNIT ACCESS LIBRARIAN STUDENT ADVISOR LIBRARY INTERN				
	5	4	3	2	1
			SALARY STEPS		

on professional tasks than at present. In future, there should be five classifications of librarian positions, including the following:

- Chief Resource Librarian
- Library Instructor
- Instructional Program Coordinator
- Archivist
- Preservation Officer
- Current Awareness Consultant
- Resource Librarian (Subject)
- Bibliographer (Form)
- Chief Cataloger
- Head, Access Services Department
- Head, Instructional Materials and Services Department
- Supervising Librarian
- Staff Development Officer
- Staff Relations Officer
- Cataloger (Subject)
- Cataloger (Serials)
- Head, Library Research and Analysis Unit
- Access Librarian
- Student Advisor
- Library Intern

The distribution of these positions among the five proposed grades is shown in Exhibit 36. As the exhibit reflects, the top two librarian classes overlap into the lower range of executive positions. Exhibit 37 lists recommended librarian positions and responsibilities that should be assigned to them.

EXHIBIT 37 (1)

Columbia University

RECOMMENDED LIBRARIAN POSITIONS
BY CLASSIFICATION

Position Title	Position Classification	Major Responsibilities
Chief Resource Librarian	L-5	Professional performance as resource librarian in a particular department (e.g., Science Department). Prepares programs and staff plans to meet established collection development, reference, and research objectives.
Library Instructor	L-5	Teaching library research methods and pursuing effective use of library resources by university teaching faculty.
Instructional Program Coordinator	L-4	Planning and operating projects which facilitate the use of the library as a teaching laboratory. This may include assisting faculty in curriculum development, coordinating classroom lectures, and providing advice and counsel on particular programs.
Archivist	L-4	Supervision of university archives, provision of in-depth reference and research services, and collection development and maintenance activities.
Preservation Officer	L-4	Coordination of a system-wide approach to the identification and processing of materials requiring preservation decisions in terms of binding, reprinting, microfilming, xeroxing, or withdrawing. Provides technical advice and guidance on specific preservation problems to individual operating units.
Current Awareness Consultant	L-4	Planning, developing, and coordinating the operation of manual and automated current awareness services provided to the faculty and designed to assist all members of the academic community in keeping abreast of new knowledge in their respective specialties.
Resource Librarian (Subject)	L-3/4	Providing, within a subject specialty, advanced reference and research services on a referral basis, collection development and preservation decisions, and, when appropriate, original cataloging support. Position involves a primary obligation to relate library resources and services to specific academic units and faculty.

EXHIBIT 37 (2)

Position Title	Position Classification	Major Responsibilities
Bibliographer (Form)	L-3/4	Acting as a selection officer for a form of material such as microforms, serials, documents, and rare books. Occasionally this position will encompass selection within a subject area which requires special language skills. Selection duties include identifying required materials, making preservation decisions, and monitoring the flow of acquisitions.
Chief Cataloger	L-3/4	Supervision of bibliographic control units and performance of advanced cataloging
Head, Access Services Department	L-3/4	Administration of circulation, information, catalog assistance, interlibrary loan, and reading room activities within a subject center.
Head, Instructional Materials and Services Department	L-2/3	Administration of reserve and duplicate collections developed to support undergraduate and graduate course requirements within subject centers. Supervision of student counseling and advisory service is also part of this position's responsibility.
Supervising Librarian	L-2/3	Supervision of staff units performing support functions, such as bibliographic searching, catalog maintenance, or record processing.
Staff Development Officer	L-2/3	Assisting the Assistant University Librarian for Personnel in the design and conduct of staff training programs for professional, specialist, and clerical staff. This position provides assistance and counseling in individual staff career planning problems.
Staff Relations Officer	L-2/3	Maintenance of viable working relationships with the clerical union within the negotiated contract and established university policies. This includes working with supervisors and union representatives to assure compliance with the terms of the contract, providing grievance assistance, and assisting university officials in negotiations.

EXHIBIT 37 (3)

Position Title	Position Classification	Major Responsibilities
Cataloger (Subject)	L-2/3	Organization and bibliographic control of library collections in specific subject areas, including creation of original catalog records, participation in the formulation of cataloging procedures and policies, and evaluation of available or proposed access points. Work includes participation in resource development and utilization areas, as appropriate.
Cataloger (Serials)	L-2/3	Completing advanced cataloging requirements for serials and advising on the organization and operation of routine serial cataloging.
Head, Library Research and Analysis Unit	L-1/3	Supervision of a research unit or analysis unit requiring a high level of technical proficiency.
Access Librarian	L-1/3	Supervisory responsibility for provision of access or instruction services within subject center, e.g., of the Information and Catalog Assistance Unit.
Student Advisor	L-1/2	Provision of direct individualized assistance in the use of library resources and services aimed particularly at helping students and other library users within a subject center.
Library Intern	L-1	Provision of access or instruction services within subject center. The position does not have supervisory responsibility and is intended to provide short-term experience to the novice librarian.

Specialist Positions

A variety of specialist positions should be established and filled by trained personnel who may not be qualified as professional librarians. These positions, which have traditionally—though unnecessarily—been filled by librarians, encompass responsibilities and skills ranging between clerical activity and advanced professional pursuits. The specialist positions are distributed among five position grades and include the following:

- Catalog Specialist
- Head, Business Services Unit
- Language Specialist
- Subject Specialist
- Accountant
- Supervisor (Allied Library Service Unit)
- Supervisor (Support or Service Activity)
- Information Specialist
- Programmer
- Reading Room Attendant
- Circulation Specialist
- Binder
- Specialist Trainee
- Personnel Assistant

The distribution of these positions among the suggested specialist grades is presented in Exhibit 38. Recommended specialist positions and responsibilities are listed in Exhibit 39.

Clerical Positions

The plan for clerical and general assistance staff should remain as in present university and union arrangements. Recent efforts have been made to establish a clerical job classification, description, and salary administration system. Clerical positions are presently defined in the personnel manual and in union contracts to encompass nine grades, as shown in Exhibit 40.

The two highest clerical classifications overlap the two lowest specialist classifications in recognition of the fact that the most

SPECIALIST POSITIONS

POSITION CLASSIFICATION	LIBRARIAN POSITIONS				

S–5	CATALOG SPECIALIST HEAD, BUSINESS SERVICES UNIT LANGUAGE SPECIALIST SUBJECT SPECIALIST ACCOUNTANT SUPERVISOR (ALLIED LIBRARY SERVICE UNIT) SUPERVISOR (SUPPORT OR SERVICE ACTIVITY)
S–4	LANGUAGE SPECIALIST SUBJECT SPECIALIST ACCOUNTANT SUPERVISOR (ALLIED LIBRARY SERVICE UNIT) SUPERVISOR (SUPPORT OR SERVICE ACTIVITY) INFORMATION SPECIALIST PROGRAMMER
S–3	SUPERVISOR (ALLIED LIBRARY SERVICE UNIT) SUPERVISOR (SUPPORT OR SERVICE ACTIVITY) PROGRAMMER READING ROOM ATTENDANT

CLERICAL POSITIONS

S–2	PROGRAMMER READING ROOM ATTENDANT CIRCULATION SPECIALIST BINDER
S–1	READING ROOM ATTENDANT SPECIALIST TRAINEE PERSONNEL ASSISTANT

5	4	3	2	1

SALARY STEPS

EXHIBIT 39 (1)

Columbia University

RECOMMENDED SPECIALIST POSITIONS
BY CLASSIFICATION

Position Title	Position Classification	Major Responsibilities
Catalog Specialist	S-5	Provision of first- and second-line reader services, such as bibliographic and catalog assistance, ready reference, directory assistance, and general information within a subject center. In addition, this position has a referral responsibility and assists in interlibrary loan transactions.
Head, Business Services Unit	S-5	Supervisor of a business-related support activity, such as fiscal control, supplies and equipment, or building maintenance.
Language Specialist	S-4/5	Performance of acquisition, bibliographic searching, and reader assistance in a specific language area such as Slavic or Japanese.
Subject Specialist	S-4/5	Performance of elementary reader services, such as location of materials, ready reference, and referral in a subject area such as biology or fine arts.
Accountant	S-4/5	Development and operation of a system of accounts which is consistent with university and library requirements. This position supervises financial services, maintains required reports, and provides technical counsel and advice.
Supervisor (Allied Library Service Unit)	S-3/5	Operation of day-to-day activities within a small reader service library unit providing information, referral assistance, supervision of staff, and materials processing support.
Supervisor (Support or Service Activity)	S-3/5	Supervision of general assistants and other clerical staff in either support units or service areas.
Information Specialist	S-4	Provision of elementary reader services, including general information, directions, directory assistance, and ready reference within a subject center.
Programmer	S-2/4	Development, operation, and maintenance of computer programs for library systems.
Reading Room Attendant	S-1/3	Supervision and maintenance of self-service units within a subject center such as microform room, periodical room, and study room.

EXHIBIT 39 (2)

Position Title	Position Classification	Major Responsibilities
Circulation Specialist	S-2	Circulation of library materials, including explanation of library rules, regulations, and procedures and the interpretation of library files and records.
Binder	S-2	Repair of library materials, supervision of processing materials requiring preservation attention, and technical advice on the maintenance of collections
Specialist Trainee	S-1	Provisional position during first six months accorded individual who is being prepared to assume one of the several specialist positions cited.
Personnel Assistant	S-1	Maintaining personnel records, assisting the assistant librarian in coordinating evaluation schedules, and keeping files of minutes.

EXHIBIT 40

COLUMBIA UNIVERSITY

RECOMMENDED STRUCTURE OF
CLERICAL POSITIONS*

GRADE LEVEL	SPECIALIST POSITIONS				
C–9		SUPERVISOR			
C–8		SUPERVISOR PERSONNEL ASSISTANT			
C–7		SUPERVISOR			
C–6		BIBLIOGRAPHIC ASSISTANT VI SECRETARY LIBRARY ASSISTANT VI LIBRARY OFFICER ASSISTANT			
C–5		BIBLIOGRAPHIC ASSISTANT V SECRETARY LIBRARY ASSISTANT V TECHNICAL ASSISTANT V LIBRARY OFFICER ASSISTANT			
C–4		BIBLIOGRAPHIC ASSISTANT IV LIBRARY ASSISTANT IV TECHNICAL ASSISTANT IV			
C–3		CLERICAL ASSISTANT III TECHNICAL ASSISTANT III			
C–2		CLERICAL ASSISTANT II TECHNICAL ASSISTANT II			
C–1		CLERICAL ASSISTANT I TECHNICAL ASSISTANT I			
	5	4	3	2	1
			SALARY STEPS		

* Based on present class titles and grade levels for local 1199 supporting staff positions grade I through VI

senior and productive clerical employees will be at least as valuable
to the libraries as the more junior workers in the specialist category.

Considerable staff study will need to be given to implementation
of the proposed staffing approaches. Ultimately the plan should
reflect defined positions based on precise work measurements experienced in the recommended organization. An illustrative staffing
plan for the new organization is presented for consideration in Exhibit
41. While the plan will require considerable redistribution of staff
among new types of positions, the overall level of staffing should
not be significantly altered.

Changing Mix of Staff

Columbia's libraries currently have a total of 532 professional and
support staff members. The optimum staffing plan recommended
in Exhibit 41 calls for a total of 541, with a net reduction of 22
in the number of executives and librarians and an increase of 48
specialists. Some 18 clerical positions are also discontinued. Thus,
the optimum plan calls for a net increase of only 9 people based
on estimates of current work loads as redistributed among the proposed organization. This increase is due in part to the need for
added staff for the new International Affairs Library and for greater
capabilities in personnel, planning, and other areas. The shift in
staffing under the optimum plan is summarized in the table that
follows.

COMPARISON OF PRESENT AND RECOMMENDED STAFFING PLANS

Positions	Present Plan	Recommended Plan	Change
Executive and Librarian	153.00	131.50	(21.50)
Specialist	10.25	58.00	47.75
Clerical	368.75	351.25	(17.50)
Total	532.00	540.75	8.75

Exhibit 42 compares the proposed staffing plan with the distribution of staff under the present plan.

The financial implications of the proposed plan will depend heavily on the salary and other decisions that are made. In summary, the long-term major implications include the following:

- Bringing existing positions into conformance with the classification scheme may increase total compensation costs as salary disparities are brought into line.
- Some savings may be anticipated due to the decreased number of librarians and the assumption that specialists will earn somewhat less per position.

Budget considerations are certain to have a direct bearing on how completely optimum staffing levels can be adopted. However, substantial improvements can be achieved by implementing the top-management executive and librarian positions as a start. The plan will provide the libraries with greater flexibility for assigning professional resources staff among several units as and when they are required.

Plan of Implementation

The recommended staffing plan will require at least one to two years to implement fully. The proposed redistribution of positions and types of positions will be difficult to accomplish due to the number of librarian positions to be dropped and the number of new specialist positions to be filled. Such adjustment as is made will require time out of consideration for professional staff and for the selection and preparation of specialists. Effective redeployment will also necessitate careful orientation of staff throughout the system as well as thorough implementation planning in advance.

This chapter has proposed a plan of staffing that should be adopted to meet the requirements of the proposed plan of organization. The next chapter recommends steps that should be taken to improve management practices and approaches to strengthen library effectiveness.

EXHIBIT 41 (1)

Columbia University

ILLUSTRATIVE NEW PLAN OF STAFFING

Organization Unit	Position Title
OFFICE OF THE VICE PRESIDENT AND UNIVERSITY LIBRARIAN	
	Vice President and University Librarian
	Support Staff
PERSONNEL OFFICE	
	Assistant University Librarian for Personnel
	Staff Development Officer
	Staff Relations Officer
	Personnel Assistant
	Support Staff
PLANNING OFFICE	
. Library Analysis Unit	Assistant University Librarian for Planning
. Operations Research Unit	Support Staff
	Manager
	Support Staff
	Library Systems Analyst (Head)
	Research Analyst (Head)
SERVICES GROUP	
Associate University Librarian's Office	
	Associate University Librarian for Services
	Support Staff
Humanistic and Historical Studies Center	
. Director's Office	Director
. Instructional Materials and Services Department	Head, Instructional Materials and Services Department
- Duplicate Collections Library	Circulation Specialist (Attendant)
	Support Staff
- Reserve Services Reading Room	Supervisor (Attendant)
	Support Staff
- Student Advisory Unit	Library Intern
. Access Services Department	Head, Access Services Department
- Microform Reading Room	Attendant
	Support Staff
- Documents Room	Attendant
	Support Staff
- Periodical Reading Room	Supervisor (Attendant)
	Support Staff
- Circulation Unit	Circulation Specialist
	Supervisor
	Supervisor (Night)
	Supervisor (Stack)
	Support Staff
- Paterno Library	Attendant and Support Staff

Position Classification	Number of Positions				
	Total	Executive	Librarian	Specialist	Clerical
	2	1			1
E-5	1	1			
C-6	1				1
	7.50	1	2	1	3.50
E-3	1	1			
L-3	1		1		
L-3	1		1		
S-1	1			1	
C-6	3.50				3.50
	7.50	2	3.50		2
E-3	1	1			
C-6	1	1			1
E-1	1				
C-5	1				1
L-3	2.50		2.50		
L-4	1		1		
	2	1			1
E-4	1	1			
C-6	1				1
	112.75	1	6.50	16	89.25
E-1	1	1			
L-2/3	1		1		
S-2	1			1	
	9				9
S-3	1			1	
	12				12
S-5 or L-1	1			1	
L-3/4	1		1		
S-3	1			1	
	1.50				1.50
S-3	1			1	
	1				1
C-7	1				1
	3.50				3.50
S-4	1			1	
S-3	1			1	
C-7	1				1
C-8	1				1
	35				35
	1.25				1.25

EXHIBIT 41 (2)

Organization Unit	Position Title
- Information and Catalog Assistance Unit	Access Librarian
	Library Intern
	Catalog Specialist
	Information Specialist
	Support Staff
- Interlibrary Loan Services Unit	Access Librarian
	Catalog Specialist
	Support Staff
. Fine Arts Library	Supervising Librarian
	Circulation Specialist
	Support Staff
. Music Library	Resource Librarian
	Supervisor
	Support Staff
. Library Service Library	Supervisor
	Support Staff
. Speech Recording Library	Supervisor
Social Science Center	
. Director's Office	Director
. Instructional Materials and Services Department	
- Reserve Reading Room	Library Intern (Attendant)
	Support Staff
- Student Advisory Unit	Library Intern (Attendant)
	Support Staff
. Access Services Department	Head, Access Services Department
- University Map Room	Librarian
- Microform Reading Room	Supervisor (Attendant)
- Periodical Reading Room	Supervisor (Attendant)
- Circulation Unit	Circulation Specialist
	Support Staff
- Information and Catalog Assistance Unit	Access Librarian
	Information Specialist
- Interlibrary Loan Services Unit	Catalog Specialist (Librarian)
. Business and Economics Library	Supervising Librarian
	Circulation Specialist
	Information Specialist
	Catalog Specialist
	Supervisor
	Support Staff
. Social Work Library	Supervisor
	Support Staff
. Journalism Library	Resource Librarian
	Supervisor
	Support Staff
. Ware Library	City Planner

Position Classification	Number of Positions				
	Total	Executive	Librarian	Specialist	Clerical
L-2	1		1		
L-1	1		1		
S-5	2			2	
S-4	2			2	
	1.50				1.50
L-1	1		1		
S-5	1			1	
	4				4
L-2	0.50 to 0.75		0.50 to 0.75		
S-2	1			1	
	4.50				4.50
L-4	1		1		
S-3	1			1	
	5.50				5.50
S-5	1			1	
	7.50				7.50
S-2	1			1	
	52	1	4	11	36
E-1	1	1			
S-4 or L-1	0.50			0.50	
	0.50				0.50
S-4 or L-1	0.50			0.50	
	0.50				0.50
L-3/4	1		1		
S-3	1			1	
C-8	1				1
C-8	1				1
S-2	1			1	
	4				4
L-1	1		1		
S-4	1			1	
S-5	1			1	
L-2	1		1		
S-2	1			1	
S-4	1			1	
S-5	1			1	
S-1	1			1	
	20				20
S-4	1			1	
	5				5
L-4	1		1		
C-8	1				1
	3				3
S-1	1			1	

EXHIBIT 41 (3)

Organization Unit	Position Title
Science Information Center	
. Director's Office	Director
. Instructional Materials and Services Department	Head, Instructional Materials and Services Department
- Reserve Reading Room	Support Staff
- Current Awareness Service Unit	
- Student Advisory Unit	
. Access Services Department	Head, Access Services Department
- Interlibrary Loan Services Unit	
- Circulation Unit	Circulation Specialist
	Support Staff
- Information and Catalog Assistance Unit	
- Technical Reports Unit	
. Biological Sciences Library	Supervisor
	Support Staff
. Physics Library	Supervisor
	Support Staff
. Mathematics Library	Supervisor
	Support Staff
. Lamont Geological Observatory Library	Supervisor
	Support Staff
. Chemistry Library	Supervisor
	Support Staff
. Psychology Library	Supervisor
	Support Staff
. Geology Library	Supervisor
	Support Staff
LAW LIBRARY CENTER	
. Director's Office	Director
	Secretary
. Access Services Department	Circulation Specialist (Head)
	Support Staff
. Instructional Materials Department	Student Advisor (Head)
	Support Staff
. Resource Development and Utilization Department	Resource Librarian (Head) [includes International Law]
	Bibliographer
	Support Staff
. International Law Library	Circulation Specialist
	Support Staff
MEDICAL SCIENCE INFORMATION CENTER	
. Director's Office	Director
	Support Staff
. Access Services Department	Supervisor (Head)
	Support Staff
. Instructional Materials Department	Student Advisor (Head)
	Support Staff

Position Classification	Number of Positions				
	Total	Executive	Librarian	Specialist	Clerical
	33	1	1	7	24
E-1	1	1			
L-2,3	0.50		0.50		
	2				2
L-2	0.50		0.50		
S-2	1			1	
	5				5
S-5	1			1	
	2.25				2.25
S-5	1			1	
	2.25				2.25
S-5	1			1	
	2.50				2.50
S-5	1			1	
	1.75				1.75
S-5	1			1	
	2.50				2.50
S-5	1			1	
	2.25				2.25
S-5	1			1	
	2.50				2.50
	28.25	1	6.25	2	19
E-4	1	1			
C-5	1				1
S-2	1			1	
	7				7
L-1	1		1		
	4				4
L-3,4,5	4.25		4.25		
L-3	1		1		
	5				5
S-2	1			1	
	2				2
	30.25	1	11.75	2	15.50
E-4	1	1			
C-5	1				1
S-1	1			1	
	6 '				6
L-1	1		1		
	3.50				3.50

EXHIBIT 41 (4)

Organization Unit	Position Title
. Resource Development and Utilization Department	Resource Librarian (Head)
	Bibliographer
	Supervisor
	Support Staff
. Affiliated Hospital Libraries	Supervising Librarian
DISTINCTIVE COLLECTIONS	
. University Archival Collections	Archivist
. Manuscripts and Rare Books Collections	Director
	Resource Librarian
	Bibliographer
	Supervisor
	Support Staff
. Architecture Collections	Director
	Resource Librarian
	Bibliographer
	Supervisor
	Support Staff
. East Asian Collections	Chief Resource Librarian (Director)
	Access Librarian
	Access Librarian
	Circulation Specialist
	Support Staff
- Chinese Section	Resource Librarian
	Cataloger
	Support Staff
- Japanese Section	Resource Librarian
	Cataloger
	Support Staff
- Korean Section	Resource Librarian
	Support Staff
RESOURCES GROUP	
Associate University Librarian's Office	
	Associate University Librarian for Resources
	Support Staff
Current Awareness Programs Coordinator's Office	
	Current Awareness Programs Coordinator
	Support Staff
Instructional Programs Coordinator's Office	
	Instructional Programs Coordinator
	Support Staff

Recommended Positions

Position Classification	Total	Executive	Librarian	Specialist	Clerical
L-3,4,5	5		5		
L-3	1		1		
S-1	1			1	
	5				5
L-2	4.75		4.75		
	45.50	2	18	3	22.50
L-4	1		1		
E-2	1	1			
L-3,4,5	3		3		
L-4	1		1		
S-1	1			1	
	7				7
E-1	1	1			
L-3,4	2		2		
L-3	1		1		
S-1	1			1	
	3.50				3.50
L-5	1		1		
L-2	1		1		
L-1	1	1			
S-2	1			1	
	5				5
	1		1		
L-3	2		2		
	3				3
L-4	1		1		
L-3	2		2		
	3				3
L-4	1		1		
	1				1
	2	1			1
E-4	1	1			
C-5	1				1
	2		1		1
L-4	1		1		
C-5	1				1
	2		1		1
L-4	1		1		
C-5	1				1

EXHIBIT 41 (5)

Organization Unit	Position Title
Resource Development and Utilization Division	
. Director's Office	Director
	Support Staff
. Science Department	Chief Resource Librarian
	Support Staff
. Humanistic and Historical Studies Department	Chief Resource Librarian
	Support Staff
. Social Science Department	Chief Resource Librarian
	Support Staff
Bibliographic Control Division	
. Director's Office	Director
	Support Staff
. Science Catalogers	Chief Cataloger
	Support Staff
. Humanistic and Historical Catalogers	Chief Cataloger
	Support Staff
. Social Science Catalogers	Chief Cataloger
	Support Staff
. Medical Science Catalogers	Chief Cataloger
	Support Staff
. Law Catalogers	Chief Cataloger
	Support Staff
. Distinctive Collections Catalogers	Chief Cataloger
	Support Staff
. Language Specialists Catalogers	Cataloger
	Support Staff
SUPPORT GROUP	
Associate University Librarian's Office	
	Associate University Librarian for Support
	Support Staff
Business Services Department	
	Manager
	Support Staff
. Preservation, Binding, and Photographic Services Unit	Supervising Librarian (Head)
- Binding Section	Supervisor
	Binder
	Support Staff

Position Classification	Number of Positions				
	Total	Executive	Librarian	Specialist	Clerical
	24.00	1	18		5
E-1	1	1			
C-5	1				1
L-3,4	3		3		
	1				1
L-3,4,5	5		5		
	1				1
L-3,4,5	10		10		
	2				2
	37.00	1	23.00		13.00
E-1	1	1			
C-5	1				1
L-3	2		2		
	1				1
L-3	2		2		
	1				1
L-3,4	3		3		
	1				1
L-3	2		2		
	2				2
L-3,4	5		5		
	4				4
L-3	1		1		
	1				1
L-3,4	8		8		
	2				2
	2	1			1
E-4	1	1			
C-5	1				1
	43.50	1	2	6	33.50
E-1	1	1			
C-5	1				1
L-2	1		1		
S-1	1			1	
S-2	1			1	
	7				7

EXHIBIT 41 (6)

Organization Unit	Position Title
- Micrographic Section	Supervisor
	Support Staff
- Photographic Lab Section	Supervisor
	Support Staff
. Facilities and Supplies Unit	Supervisor (Head)
	Supervisor
	Support Staff
. Financial Services Unit	Accountant (Head)
. Data Control Unit	
- Computer Operations Section	Supervisor (Head)
	Support Staff
- Programmers Section	Automated Systems Specialist (Supervisor)
	Programmer

Records and Materials Processing Department

	Manager
	Support Staff
. Bibliographic Searching Unit	Supervising Librarian (Head)
- Acquisition Searching Section	Supervisor
	Support Staff
- Catalog Searching Section	Supervisor
	Support Staff
- Foreign Language Section	Supervisor
	Support Staff
- Gifts and Exchanges Section	Supervisor
	Support Staff
. Monographs Unit	Supervising Librarian (Head)
- Order/Receipt Section	Support Staff
- Cataloging With Copy Section	Supervisor (Head)
	Supervisor
	Support Staff
- Materials Processing Section	Supervisor
	Support Staff
. Serials Unit	Supervising Librarian (Head)
- Order/Receipt Section	Supervisor
	Support Staff
- Recording Section	Supervisor
	Catalog Specialist
	Support Staff
- Cataloging Section*	Cataloger
	Support Staff

---

* Although the performance of original serials cataloging should be the responsibility of the Bibliographic Control Division in the Resources Group, it is recommended that the serials cataloging staff initially work within the Serials Unit to establish effective operation.

Position Classification	Total	Number of Positions			
		Executive	Librarian	Specialist	Clerical
S-1	0.50			0.50	
	3.50				3.50
S-1	0.50			0.50	
	3				3
S-2	1			1	
C-7	1				1
	2				2
S-5	1			1	
S-3	1			1	
	16				16
L-4	1		1		
S-1	1			1	
	108.50	1	14.50	9	84
E-1	1	1			
C-5	1				1
L-2	1		1		
L-1	0.50		0.50		
	6				6
L-1	0.50		0.50		
	6				6
S-2	1			1	
	7				7
S-3	1			1	
	1				1
L-2	1		1		
	14				14
L-3	1		1		
S-2	1			1	
	7				7
S-1	1			1	
	7				7
L-2	1		1		
S-2	1			1	
	6				6
L-2	1		1		
S-5	1			1	
	5				5
L-3,4	4.50		4.50		
	2				2

EXHIBIT 41 (7)

Organization Unit	Position Title
. Documents Unit	Supervising Librarian (Head)
- Order/Receipt Section	Supervisor
	Support Staff
- Record Processing Section	Supervisor
	Catalog Specialist
	Support Staff
. Catalog Maintenance Unit	Supervising Librarian (Head)
- Card Production Section	Supervisor
	Support Staff
- Record Review and Filing Section	Supervisor (Head)
	Supervisor
	Support Staff
- Catalog Editing Section	Supervisor (Head)
	Support Staff
Total	—

Recommended Positions

Position Classification	Number of Positions				
	Total	Executive	Librarian	Specialist	Clerical
L-2	1		1		
S-2	1			1	
	2				2
L-1	1		1		
S-5	1			1	
	2				2
L-2	1		1		
S-3	1			1	
	11				11
L-3	0.50		0.50		
C-7	1				1
	4				4
L-3	0.50		0.50		
	2				2
	540.75	18.00	113.50	58.00	351.25

EXHIBIT 42 (1)

Columbia University

COMPARISON OF ILLUSTRATIVE AND PRESENT PLANS OF ORGANIZATION
AS OF AUGUST 12, 1971

	Recommended Plan of Staffing				
		Number of Positions			
Organization Unit	Total	Executive	Librarian	Specialist	Clerical
Office of the Vice President and University Librarian	2	1			1
Personnel Office	7.50	1	2	1	3.50
Planning Office	2	1			1
. Manager	2	1			1
. Library Analysis Unit	2.50		2.50		
. Operations Research Unit	1		1		
Services Group					
. Associate University Librarian's Office	1	1			
. Humanistic and Historical Studies Center					
- Director's Office	1	1			
- Instructional Materials and Services Department	1		1		
. Duplicate Collections Library	10			1	9
. Reserve Services Reading Room	13			1	12
. Student Advisory Unit	1			1	
- Access Services Department	1		1		
. Microform Reading Room	2.50			1	1.50
. Documents Room	2			1	1
. Periodical Reading Room	4.50				4.50
. Circulation Unit	39			2	37
. Paterno Library	1.25				1.25
. Information and Catalog Assistance Unit	7.50		2	4	1.50
. Interlibrary Loan Services Unit	6		1	1	4
- Fine Arts Library	6		0.50	1	4.50
- Music Library	7.50		1	1	5.50
- Library Service Library	8.50			1	7.50
- Speech Recording Library	1			1	
. Social Science Center					
- Director's Office	1	1			
- Instructional Materials and Services Department					
. Reserve Reading Room	1			0.50	0.50
. Student Advisory Unit	1			0.50	0.50
- Access Services Department	1		1		
. University Map Room	1			1	
. Microform Reading Room	1				1
. Periodical Reading Room	1				1
. Circulation Unit	5			1	4
. Information and Catalog Assistance Unit	2		1	1	
. Interlibrary Loan Services Unit	1			1	
- Business and Economics Library	25		1	4	20
- Social Work Library	6			1	5

Organization Unit	Number of Positions				
	Total	Executive	Librarian	Specialist	Clerical
Office of the Director and Associate Director	3.50	2			1.50
Administrative Services (Personnel, Budget, Finance)	7.50	2	1	1	3.50
Systems Office					
. Administration Section	4		2		2
. Analysis Section	2.50		2.50		
. Programming Section	2		1	1	
Units Similar to Services Group					
See Director's Office					
See Director's Office					
Butler Librarian	1	1			
. Philosophy Library	2				2
. Burgess/Carpenter Library	11		1	1	9
. Columbia College Library	14		2		12
. Microfilm Reading Room	2.50				2.50
. Periodical Reading Room	4.50				4.50
. Central Circulation Unit	40.25		2	1	37.25
. Paterno Library	1				1
. Reference Department	13.50		8		5.50
. Fine Arts Library	6.50		2		4.50
. Music Library	7.50		2		5.50
. Library Service Library	9.50		2		7.50
. Speech Recording Library	1		1		
. International Affairs Library					
- Administration	3		2		1
- Circulation and Reference Services	9		2		7
- Area Studies Bibliographic Services	15		7		8
. Business and Economics Library	24		6		18
. Social Work Library	7		2		5

Present Plan of Staffing

EXHIBIT 42 (2)

Recommended Plan of Staffing

Organization Unit		Number of Positions			
	Total	Executive	Librarian	Specialist	Clerical
- Journalism Library	5		1		4
- Ware Library	1			1	
. Science Information Center					
- Director's Office	1	1			
- Instructional Materials and Services Department	2.50		0.50		2
. Reserve Reading Room					
. Current Awareness Service Unit					
. Student Advisory Unit					
- Access Services Department	0.50		0.50		
. Interlibrary Loan Services Unit					
. Circulation Unit	6			1	5
. Information and Catalog Assistance Unit					
. Technical Reports Unit					
- Biological Sciences Library	3.25			1	2.25
- Physics Library	3.25			1	2.25
- Mathematics Library	3.50			1	2.50
- Lamont Geological Observatory Library	2.75			1	1.75
- Chemistry Library	3.50			1	2.50
- Psychology Library	3.25			1	2.25
- Geology Library	3.50			1	2.50
. Law Library Center					
- Director's Office	2	1			1
- Access Services Department	8			1	7
- Instructional Materials Department	5		1		4
- Resource Development and Utilization Department	10.25		5.25		5
- International Law Library	3			1	2
. Medical Science Information Center					
- Director's Office	2	1			1
- Access Services Department	7			1	6
- Instructional Materials Department	4.50		1		3.50
- Resource Development and Utilization Department	12		6	1	5
- Affiliated Hospital Libraries	4.75	4.75			
. Distinctive Collections					
- University Archival Collections	1		1		
- Manuscripts and Rare Books Collections	13	1	4	1	7
- Architecture Collections	8.50	1	3	1	3.50
- East Asian Collections	23		10	1	12

Organization Unit	Present Plan of Staffing				
	Number of Positions				
	Total	Executive	Librarian	Specialist	Clerical
. Journalism Library	5		1		4
. Ware Library	1.50				1.50
Engineering Library	9		2		7
. Biological Sciences Library	3.25		1		2.25
. Physics Library	3.25		1		2.25
. Mathematics Library	3.50		1		2.50
. Lamont Upper Mantle	2.75		1		1.75
. Chemistry Library	3.50		1		2.50
. Psychology Library	4.50		1		3.50
. Geology Library	4.50		1		3.50
Law Division	2	1			1
. Reference	3.25		3.25		
. International Law	4		1		3
. Acquisitions Section	6		1		5
. Circulation Section	6		1		5
. Student Assistants	9.50				9.50
Medical Sciences Division					
. Administrative	5	1	1		3
. Reference	7		6		1
. Circulation Section	8			1	7
. Acquisitions Section	7		1	1	5
. Student Assistants	2.50				2.50
. Affiliated Hospital Libraries	4.75		4.75		
Special Collections Division	13.25	1			1
			4		7
				0.25	
. Columbiana	1		1		
. Avery Library	8.50		5		3.50

EXHIBIT 42 (3)

Recommended Plan of Staffing

Organization Unit	Number of Positions				
	Total	Executive	Librarian	Specialist	Clerical
Resources Group					
. Associate University Librarian's Office	2	1			1
. Current Awareness Programs Coordinator's Office	2		1		1
. Instructional Programs Coordinator's Office	2		1		1
. Resource Development and Utilization Division					
- Director's Office	2	1			1
- Science Department	4		3		1
- Humanistic and Historical Studies Department	6		5		1
- Social Science Department	12		10		2
. Bibliographic Control Division					
- Director's Office	2	1			1
- Science Catalogers	3		2		1
- Humanistic and Historical Catalogers	3		2		1
- Social Science Catalogers	4		3		1
- Medical Science Catalogers	4		2		2
- Law Catalogers	9		5		4
- Distinctive Collections Catalogers	2		1		1
- Language Specialist Catalogers	10		8		2
Support Group					
. Associate University Librarian's Office	2	1			1
. Business Services Department	2	1			1
- Preservation, Binding, and Photographic Services Unit	1		1		
. Binding Section	9			2	7
. Micrographic Section	4			0.50	3.50
. Photographic Lab Section	3.50			0.50	3
- Facilities and Supplies Unit	4			1	3
- Financial Services Unit	1		1		
- Data Control Unit					
. Computer Operations Section	17			1	16
. Programmers Section	2		1	1	

Organization Unit	Number of Positions				
	Total	Executive	Librarian	Specialist	Clerical
Units Similar to Resources Group					
Cataloging Department	22		18		4
Law Cataloging Section	9		5		4
Medical Cataloging Section	4.75		2		2.75
Central Technical Services Administration	4	1	2		1
. Binding and Preservation	9			1	8
. Photographic Services	7.50		1		6.50
. Library Office	5.50	1	1		3.50
. Shipping Room	3				3
. Data Control	20		1	2	17

EXHIBIT 42 (4)

Recommended Plan of Staffing

Organization Unit	Total	Executive	Librarian	Specialist	Clerical
. Records and Materials Processing Department	2	1			1
- Bibliographic Searching Unit	1		1		
. Acquisition Searching Section	6.50		0.50		6
. Catalog Searching Section	6.50		0.50		6
. Foreign Language Section	8			1	7
. Gifts and Exchanges Section	2			1	1
- Monographs Unit	1		1		
. Order/Receipt Section	14				14
. Cataloging With Copy Section	9		1	1	7
. Materials Processing Section	8			1	7
- Serials Unit	1		1		
. Order/Receipt Section	7			1	6
. Recording Section	7		1	1	5
. Cataloging Section *	6.50		4.50		2
- Documents Unit	1		1		
. Order/Receipt Section	3			1	2
. Record Processing Section	4		1	1	2
- Catalog Maintenance Unit	1		1		
. Card Production Section	12			1	11
. Record Review and Filing Section	5.50		0.50		5
. Catalog Editing Section	2.50		0.50		2
Total	540.75	18.00	113.50	58.00	351.25

* Although the performance of original serials cataloging should be a responsibility of the Bibliographic Control Division in the Resources Group, it is recommended that the serials cataloging staff initially work within the Serials Unit to help establish effective operation.

Organization Unit	Total	Executive	Librarian	Specialist	Clerical
		Number of Positions			
Processing Department	2		1		1
. Acquisition Searching Section	7		1		6
. Catalog Processing Section	13		1		12
. Gifts and Exchange Section	3		1		2
. Book Order Section	16		1		15
. Cataloging With Copy Section	9		1		8
. Book Processing Section	8			1	7
Serials and Documents Acquisition Section	19.50		4		15.50
Serials Cataloging Section	14.50		7.50		7
. Card Production Section	12.25		1		11.25
. See Catalog Processing Section, Catalog Department, and Cataloging With Copy Section					
	532.00	10.00	143.00	10.25	368.75

CHAPTER FOUR

Recommended Approaches to Management and Professional Activities

The way in which management and professional activities are approached is as vital to the effectiveness of Columbia's libraries as its structure of organization and patterns of staffing. The way in which the staff of the libraries—executives, librarians, specialists, and clerical staff—work together daily will determine how well the academic community will be served and how well the resources of Columbia's libraries will be developed and used.

The success of the libraries depends on the effectiveness of planning and execution of programs, formulation and use of policy and budgets, and leadership and supervision. Staff effectiveness will also be determined by how well library components work together and communicate.

The recommendations presented in this chapter set forth improvements that should be made in the management and professional activities of Columbia's libraries. Strengthened performance in these areas will be of critical importance in adopting the proposed new patterns of organization and staffing.

REQUIREMENTS OF THE FUTURE

Columbia's libraries should constantly strive to improve management approaches to meet the changing needs of the university.

Management Trends in Higher Education

Approaches to management and professional activities at Columbia's libraries are currently undergoing change. Staff members are becoming better informed about library matters and more involved in processes of decision making than in the past. Regular staff meetings are being held at all levels, and a periodic newsletter is sent out by the Director of Libraries. Committees are active in involving staff in significant library issues such as defining the nature of the professional at Columbia and evaluating meaningful approaches to staff development. The Representative Committee of Librarians has also presented a paper on peer evaluation for consideration by the libraries. In addition, new ways are being sought to maintain high performance, despite budget cutbacks, while long-range library development plans are being formulated.

Despite these innovations, additional improvements are needed to equip the libraries to respond to future needs and challenges. Many of these problems are recognized and are being addressed by the library leadership. Several areas in particular will need strengthening for the recommended plans of organization and staffing to be implemented effectively.

Changing instruction and research needs will require closer and more meaningful liaison with faculty. Freeing resources staff from many operating duties will require supervisors and staff alike to adapt to multiple reporting relationships. In addition, to enhance planning and decision-making, groups comprised of individuals crossing administrative and other lines will increasingly be needed.

*Principles of Management and
Professional Activities*

Successful management approaches demonstrated in other institutions can be embodied in principles applicable to university libraries. These principles call for:

- Logical, comprehensive, and action-oriented planning
- Meaningful processes for formulating and communicating policy
- Program-related budgets whose formulation and adoption are based on accurate information and appropriate staff input

- Effective leadership and supervision throughout the system to convey purpose and to mobilize available resources constructively
- Constructive working relationships and communication throughout the libraries
- Effective staff development plans that meet staffing requirements and help individuals achieve their personal aspirations

Columbia's libraries have demonstrated achievements in several of these areas. Improvements need to be made, however, to strengthen overall library performance in light of these principles. Means should be found to initiate comprehensive planning throughout Columbia's libraries as a guide to their own development and for presentation to university officials. Supervisory techniques will need substantial modification and reorientation under the proposed plan. Supervisors will need to develop and train their staff as well as oversee staff activities. Perhaps most benefit will be gained from concerted efforts to reinforce the personnel function at Columbia's libraries. Nearly all the management approaches recommended, particularly staff development practices, will depend on effective personnel programs for training and orientation of staff. A greater commitment of resources to the personnel function is needed for effective implementation and ongoing development. Implementing the management approaches recommended in this chapter should better equip Columbia's libraries to mobilize staff and other resources as needed to meet the university's changing requirements.

NEW APPROACHES TO MANAGEMENT AND
PROFESSIONAL ACTIVITIES

New approaches to management and professional practices should benefit the users and staff of Columbia's libraries. They should integrate and relate library human and financial resources more effectively than at present. In particular, the approaches should incorporate practices of value in other institutions in areas such as developing trained and experienced personnel, applying group problem-solving techniques, and establishing multiple reporting relationships.

Management Practices Employed Elsewhere

Over the years, in response to demands for greater cost effectiveness and improved service levels, management techniques have been strengthened in many institutions through the:

- Definition and use of executive and paraprofessional positions that permit more concerted and efficient utilization of high-cost professional talents
- Application of specialized business skills in accounting, budgeting, operations research, and cost analysis to the problems of educational, medical, and other institutions
- Provision and refinement of staff training and development programs to provide the skills needed by the institution or business
- Provision of supervisory, middle-management, and executive training programs

Similar techniques can and should be applied to the management approaches and professional practices employed in Columbia's libraries.

High Priority for Human Resources

High priority needs to be given to the effective development and utilization of the libraries' human resources not only to offer quality service to users, but also to assure meaningful opportunities for staff career fulfillment. The time and energy devoted to library recruitment and placement efforts should result in high productivity and sustained performance. However, many variables can affect an individual's interest in and commitment to his work. Experience has shown a strong correlation of high performance and low turnover with positive employee attitudes and motivation. Such considerations have equal (if not greater) validity in a professional enterprise such as the research library.

Personnel policies and practices should be designed to reinforce a constructive work environment in terms of job content and helpful work relationships. This approach is important for all staff even though professionals tend to be more vocationally oriented and self-sufficient than others. Equitable compensation, work satisfaction, sense of support for and contribution to institutional goals, and meaningful career opportunities are important factors affecting staff attitudes and performance.

Adoption of the recommended staffing plan should substantially realign positions to better focus energies and talents of professional and other staff and, hence, should help foster constructive attitudes. In addition, supervisory practices, open communication, and other techniques recommended in this chapter should enhance these staff potentialities. Employee attitudes toward supervisors, and toward the institution generally, should be monitored periodically as they constitute an important criterion for measuring the performance of those in leadership positions.

Group Problem Solving

Columbia's libraries have complex operational and decision-making requirements which make it essential that the different skills and resources needed to solve problems can be mobilized effectively. These varied skills and resources, however, are seldom available in a single position or person, and often can be obtained only through groups specially constructed for the problem at hand. Thus, for the recommended plans of organization and staffing to work well, effective construction and use of groups for problem solving will be essential.

Group problem solving does not mean abrogating the lines of authority needed for decisions to be made and actions taken. It is more than just the use of committees. It aims at drawing upon appropriate staff resources to formulate policies and programs that are relevant and based on accurate facts. It will be extremely important in the proposed plan of organization that such groups be formed as needed to bring the specialized but interrelated perspectives of resource, service, and support staff together to solve operating problems and to participate in decision making. Professional organizations frequently do not take sufficient advantage of their human resources in this manner. They expect individual staff members as professionals to act independently of one another, thereby reducing the organization's potential for achievement through collective effort.

The present structure brings division heads together for communication and decision making at several points. Periodic professional staff meetings and the efforts of the representative and standing committees have improved group participation in management at Columbia's libraries. Interviews and questionnaires, however, indicate a strong tendency among library staff to operate singly and through established administrative lines of authority rather than together for effective problem solving and planning.

The new approaches to management recommended in the following sections should enhance participation in library matters by means of effective use of technical and program advisory groups, through staff training in group dynamics, and with the leadership of the library executives and Personnel Office working closely together to coordinate the staff development and management.

Multiple Reporting Relationships

The recommended plan of organization provides for integrity in the upward reporting relationships of staff in each of the major groups—Resources, Services, and Support. Thus, plans, policies, and budgets concerning library resources will be approved by the Associate University Librarian for Resources. Similarly, service decisions will be made by the Associate University Librarian for Services. Some professional staff, however, with service and resource responsibilities will need to adjust to multiple reporting relationships according to the functional area involved. This will require sensitive negotiations between supervisory and executive staff to determine how the time of such people should be allocated. It will also necessitate setting forth explicit definitions of the policy and administrative matters which fall within each area's authority.

It should be noted, however, that the recommended staffing plan does not envisage large numbers of professional staff with split obligations. Such arrangements will occur principally among resources staff who have some administrative duties in the services areas as well as in an allied library. Multiple reporting relationships should also be used within the organizational boundaries of the major groups of Resources, Services, and Support. For example, within the Resources Group, catalogers assigned the creation of

original bibliographic records have subject skills, collection knowledge, and language abilities which should be available to the
academic community. They should be involved in regular selection
and preservation activities under the Resource Development and
Utilization Division and be included in projects such as graduate
student consultation, preparation of bibliographies, and classroom
lectures. The catalogers' immediate responsibility is the division's
work load, but possibly 20 percent of their time may be applied
to different organizational goals.

Multiple reporting relationships will give the libraries far more
staffing flexibility to meet changing requirements. Staff time can
be assigned more efficiently to conserve and apply critical professional skills as needed, sometimes crossing administrative or operating unit lines. This approach also has job enlargement benefits
for many professional staff members whose specialized training
and experience are now often wasted on nonprofessional activities.

High Performance Goals

Planning is given greater emphasis in the new approaches to management for Columbia's libraries. Planning is essential for reaching
rational decisions and judgments about present and future development whether in periods of growth or retrenchment. For the
immediate future, it is almost certain that few added resources will
be available for improvements to be made; therefore, needed change
will have to be accomplished by adjustment of present library
capabilities. Effective planning will require meaningful performance
goals to be established as a basis for evaluating alternatives and
monitoring levels of achievement. Such measures, though not currently available for use at Columbia's libraries, are vital for monitoring performance in the future.

Initially, performance measures for the university libraries might
be classified in four categories: elapsed time, user satisfaction, cost
effectiveness, and staff attitudes and development. Each operating
unit should establish performance measures in each category for
use in program evaluation and verification and in budget submis-
sions. The measures adopted should be reviewed periodically and
improved as experience is gained and in light of changing needs

of the university and the libraries. Several illustrative applications of the performance principle are suggested here; however, to have real credibility and staff acceptance and commitment, these measures should be formulated by those directly responsible for the activities to be measured and should be approved by management.

Elapsed time as a performance measurement approach has particular relevance in areas such as materials acquisition, processing, circulation, and other services where speed in completing a transaction is the critical factor. Staff and users now informally evaluate performance in these vital activities in terms of, e.g., how long it takes for a book order to be placed and filled. The proposed organization was in part designed (with respect to bibliographic searching, monographs, serials, and documents) to isolate self-contained activities to facilitate the assessment of performance and more effectively centralize responsibility.

Though often difficult to ascertain, user patterns and satisfaction are important performance measures. The system-wide user and cost survey completed in 1969–1970 by Columbia staff was very useful in categorizing the nature of library use (instructional versus research) and assigning costs. Circulation figures help measure only a limited aspect of library service. User attitudes and utilization of the libraries (e.g., reference, browsing, study, or research) should be sampled periodically by each operating unit. Computer capabilities may be developed in the near future that will permit library staff to determine circulation patterns by title and subject area. Such information, which is presently unavailable, might point to new physical arrangements that would expedite faculty and student access to frequently used materials.

Strengthened relations with faculty should prove an important source for determining user satisfaction with the proposed library Services and Resources Groups. The primary purpose of this faculty relationship is, of course, to assure the satisfactory development of library resources to meet the academic needs of the university. In another sense, however, faculty relations also provide an important vehicle for communicating general user attitudes and needs.

Cost-benefit comparisons between program and staffing alternatives are likely to be increasingly important measures of performance, particularly in view of university-wide financial considerations. However, much study must be undertaken before adequate unit cost information is available for analysis at Columbia's libraries or elsewhere. As a first step efforts should be made to allocate all associated costs among the major programs of the library and to relate these costs to the specific services rendered and their benefits.

The notion of cost performance measures requires careful application. The least costly service or method may also be the least satisfactory for other reasons. Knowing the real costs of basic programs will better enable the management of Columbia's libraries to establish optimum priorities for achieving the best quality and mix of services at the lowest cost. The proposed functional division—services, resources, and support—reflects three basic library programs that compete for funds and represent real choices (e.g., more reader services, more collections, or more records). This division should also help to accumulate real cost experience and highlight choices and their implications.

Staff attitudes and patterns throughout the system also provide valuable guides to performance. Alert supervisors and executives should be sensitive to changes in staff attitudes and be prepared to take appropriate action. Formal means of assessing this indicator of performance should be developed, including the monitoring of staff turnover, promotions, disciplinary problems, applications for employment, and reasons for staff departures. Consideration should also be given to periodic application of established attitude surveys, such as the Likert Profile of Organizational Characteristics. These surveys provide detailed information on how staff members view critical aspects of management, such as leadership styles, decision-making patterns, communications, goal setting, and performance objectives. Such surveys can detect trends and problems that need attention if the full potentials of the libraries are to be fulfilled.

APPROACH TO LIBRARY PLANNING

The Columbia library system should approach planning as a means of controlling its own destiny in the context of the university as a whole. University plans, as they are developed, and library plans should be carefully interrelated. The Vice President and University Librarian should establish active liaison with appropriate university officials for purposes of planning. The proposed Planning Office provides Columbia's libraries with the capability of developing and updating meaningful plans consistent with changing university requirements.

Planning Format and Schedule

The planning function at Columbia's libraries should be comprehensive, systematic, scheduled, action-oriented, and based on accurate information. It should be carried out at each level of the library system, and standardized plan formats should be integrated into a single comprehensive plan. Essentially, the plan should define for each unit or system:

- Objectives
- Resource, service, and support programs (including plans for collection and other resource development)
- Organization
- Staffing
- Facilities
- Financing
- External and cooperative relationships (including those with regional, national, and international library enterprises)

Plans adopted should draw upon the efforts of appropriate individuals and units throughout the system. The Vice President and University Librarian and his top management team should suggest the overall priorities and objectives for library development and identify emerging trends and university requirements for the next five years or more. Individual service centers and resource divisons should reflect these targets and trends in the specific plans they submit. Formal plans should be submitted annually and should include plans for the next academic year and for the next three to five years.

Assistant University Librarian
for Planning

The Assistant University Librarian for Planning should coordinate
and give professional leadership to the planning process. He should
establish planning schedules and guidelines, assemble basic information and data needed for planning, and identify bases for evaluation.
He should also relate strongly to the Operations Research Unit
for purposes of establishing and evaluating unit costs and benefits.
His office should work closely with key faculty groups and university
officials to help monitor changing needs. He should also assume
a training role, in collaboration with the Personnel Office, to prepare
system and unit officials to develop meaningful individual plans.
A major responsibility of the Planning Office should be to consolidate
individual unit plans into an overall comprehensive library plan
which can be submitted to the university by the Vice President
and University Librarian for approval and funding.

Short- and Long-Term Plans

Time and detailed preparation are fundamental to achieving desired
change. Long-term plans (three to five years) should be adopted
as the guiding framework in which annual detailed implementation
plans can be made. Columbia's libraries, through the Planning
Office, should establish a "plan for planning" to guide planning
efforts throughout the system and to keep them on schedule. The
plan should conform to the sequences and requirements of university
planning and budgeting. It should help staff order and document
their development plans in practical terms so that, once adopted,
they will provide meaningful direction for implementation. Budgeting information needed within short- and long-term plans should
also be identified and high priority should be given to integration
of program and budget plans. Consistency in planning and the need
to compare programs and costs meaningfully for decision making
will necessitate installing and using standard planning formats of
parallel construction for both short- and long-term plans.

While annual program plans and budgets should be based on
long-range plans, the latter will necessarily be affected by current

progress and experience. Accordingly, each year library staff under the leadership of the Planning Office should formally evaluate progress against goals. The results of the evaluation (e.g., problems, difficulties, and successes) should be compared with assumptions underlying plans for the following year and for the long term so that appropriate modifications can be made. Thus, short- and long-term plans for Columbia's libraries will reflect an ongoing dynamic process for setting long-range targets and translating these targets into annual implementation plans and budgets.

Participation in Planning

Appropriate people should be involved in the ongoing planning process so that all relevant knowledge, insight, and viewpoints are taken into account and reflected in the plans finally adopted. A major responsibility of the Planning Office, in consultation with the top management team, will be to design and schedule the flow of events that will achieve constructive involvement in planning. The Vice President and University Librarian and the Associate and Assistant University Librarians together should be the staff primarily responsible for formulating, reviewing, and agreeing upon library plans to be submitted to university officials. Formally, of course, the comprehensive plan should be submitted by the Vice President and University Librarian as the chief executive accountable for library affairs.

Participation in reviewing and contributing to the development of system-wide and individual unit plans should be both formal and informal. Individuals should be identified and formally involved in the planning process representing (1) university administration, faculty, and students, (2) library administration and professional and support staff, and (3) professional and technical sources outside the university.

The Executive Vice President for Academic Affairs and Provost and his key staff should be involved early and throughout the planning process to provide the university context in which library plans should be made. Selected faculty members with whom formal liaison has been established by the libraries in the services and resources areas should be consulted to review draft plans affecting them.

Similar efforts should be undertaken with appropriate student representatives.

Within the library system, the top management team, in consultation with the Planning Office, should devise means for involving its respective program and technical advisory groups in reviewing plans when their viewpoints would be useful. Similarly, the Representative Committee of Librarians and the Professional Advisory Committee should review and comment on proposed system-wide plans; adequate time should be provided for their contribution to be meaningful.

Informal means of involving staff and others in planning should also be provided. Draft plans should be available for interested individual staff members to study. Summaries of highlights of the proposed plans should be distributed widely through use of the Vice President and University Librarian's newsletter or by other means. The Vice President and University Librarian should make a presentation annually at the professional staff meeting to explain and answer questions about proposed plans, once they are near completion.

Meaningful participation in planning should be of significant benefit to Columbia's Libraries. It will assure both that plans are based on accurate information and that staff can understand and, through their participation, become committed to accomplishing the goals established. Interviews during the study and the results of a Likert questionnaire administered on a test basis to a voluntary sample of library staff indicate strong staff support for participation in all library matters where their contribution is sincerely sought.

Action-Oriented Plans

Columbia's library plans should be action oriented. They should be sufficiently concrete that, once decisions are made, it is evident what broadly needs to be done to carry them out. Estimating manpower and financial requirements for each element of the long- and short-term plans adopted will be important to assure that they are realistic and action oriented. Once plans are formally adopted, those responsible for implementing them should immediately identify specific action steps. The plans and the implementation steps and schedules established should be modified to reflect the progress actually made as implementation proceeds and experience is gained.

The complex nature of the organization, facilities, services, and user patterns of Columbia's libraries makes it imperative that clear policies be established and communicated effectively throughout the system. Library policies shoûld be carefully correlated with those of the university. They should be comprehensive and well thought out, and should reflect the deliberations of appropriate parties.

Formal Working Guides

Policies constitute formally adopted statements that govern operations. Accordingly, appropriate policies should be set for each area of significance to the libraries. They should provide staff with a framework for administrative conduct, working and reporting relationships, user privileges, and relations to users. Concise, well-organized, indexed policies will also be extremely helpful for orienting staff to new positions of responsibility and for guiding implementation over the next few years as new organization and staffing patterns and complex working relationships are tested and modified.

A necessary distinction should be made between policies and procedures. Policies are governing statements of general importance to the entire system, while procedures set forth the best way to carry out specific activities or duties. In the proposed plan for Columbia's libraries, policies typically should be formulated and adopted by the Vice President and University Librarian and his top management team. These statements should encompass areas such as:

- User privileges of Columbia faculty, undergraduate and graduate students, alumni, and families; faculty and students from affiliated institutions; and other non-Columbia users.
- Use of and access to library resources, e.g., loan of materials; open stack browsing; use of reading rooms, special collections,

etc.; access to machine-readable data bases; and use of in-depth reference and research assistance
- Charges and fees for overdue loans, specialized services to Columbia and non-Columbia users, interlibrary loans, etc.
- Personnel matters, including staff appraisals, career opportunities, notification of position openings, grievance procedures, opportunities for continuing education, etc.
- Collection development, including ordering and acquisitions, preservation, levels of excellence sought, etc.
- Planning and budgeting, e.g., approaches to and sequences for planning and budgeting, objectives for involving staff and others in the processes adopted, and authorization needed for departure from adopted plans and budgets

Policy Formulation

Policies should reflect university positions affecting the libraries and their use, as well as incorporate positions taken by the leadership of the libraries. Accordingly, in the final analysis, library policies should be set by executive staff and conveyed throughout the system by a policy manual or other devices that can be updated readily. In formulating library policy, however, all staff members who are cognizant of and knowledgeable about the issues involved and who can contribute to resolving these issues should have an opportunity for involvement. The principal focal point for this participation should be the Representative Committee of Librarians and the Professional Advisory Committee. Proposed policies should also be posted, however, to broaden the sense and substance of involvement and to foster understanding and commitment.

Regular Formal Review

Policies should be formally reviewed and updated annually. Overall responsibility for consolidating policies into a policy manual and for coordinating annual efforts to review current policies should be assigned to the Assistant University Librarian for Planning. In addition, the Vice President and University Librarian should assign responsibility for the enforcement of policies to key staff throughout the plan of organization. These staff members should be expected to review regularly the adequacy of existing policy statements and to formulate needed change.

BUDGET FORMULATION AND USE

Columbia's libraries should use budgets first to express plans in financial terms and then to control library expenditures during the budget period. In the past, the libraries have achieved the distinction of performing effectively with tight budgeting procedures, accurate and timely financial reports, and interrelated university budgets and library budgets.

In the future, budgets should increasingly be used as tools for involving key library administrators in planning and determining library priorities. In addition, the use of program budgeting should also facilitate planning and performance evaluation.

Planning and Budgeting

The importance of integrated planning and budgeting and of decentralized budget formulation and control responsibilities cannot be exaggerated. Without explicit cost information, program plans are abstract and accurate decisions cannot be reached. Responsible operating officials must have major roles in developing plans and budgets if they are to be held accountable for performance in their units. More importantly, their involvement will assure greater accuracy in estimating costs and assessing the implications of alternative plans and budgets for individual programs and services. In addition, it will develop the staff's management capabilities in terms of relating programs and costs and becoming more conscious of cost effectiveness.

Assistant University Librarian for Planning

The Assistant University Librarian for Planning should serve the Vice President and University Librarian as chief budget officer. He should meet with top executives as part of a regular annual cycle to present and explain university and library budget guidelines and priorities and to establish a schedule for submission and review of budget requests. He should develop and use a standard budget format which is compatible with the university's plans and with the short- and long-term plans of the libraries. Following submission of preliminary budget requests, he should meet with each Associate and Assistant University Librarian to review and clarify budget requests and to reconcile inconsistencies with established guidelines. Once modified budget requests and justifications are submitted by each executive, the Assistant University Librarian for Planning should prepare a consolidated library budget summary for the Vice President and University Librarian to review. The budget summary should include a comparative analysis of the unit budget requests and the planning officer's recommended overall budget together with his justifications. The consolidated budget must then be thoroughly reviewed and approved by the Vice President and University Librarian before being submitted to the university administration.

It will be essential for the Assistant University Librarian for Planning to establish close ties with his counterparts in the university, since it will be primarily his responsibility to see that library plans and budgets are compatible with approaches, schedules, and formats of the university. These ties should also place him in a position to influence the university when the libraries develop more effective planning and budgeting approaches.

Program Budgets

A program budget approach should be developed for use in Columbia's libraries to better define and interpret the complex operations of the library system and to relate them to costs for meaningful control and evaluation. A fully tested program budget design has not yet been developed for research libraries, although it is a matter of active current interest and study. Implementation of the proposed organization should provide Columbia's libraries with a significant opportunity for leadership in the budgeting area. In particular, this leadership could be expressed through:

- Development of comprehensive short- and long-term plans that incorporate detailed cost and financial information
- Adoption of program definitions of the precise service and activity areas that comprise the work of the libraries and identification of their respective cost components
- Meaningful interpretation of library costs in terms of the major programs of the university (e.g., instruction, research, undergraduate, and graduate)
- Adoption of specific program and budget goals and development of cost performance measures to relate costs to services provided

A sophisticated program budget approach will require substantial time and effort to develop and will depend on successful implementation of the organization and staffing recommendations. However, Columbia's libraries can make significant progress in program budgeting in the near future.

The proposed plan of organization provides the basic outline for assigning costs and preparing budgets along broad functional lines of resources, services, support, personnel, and planning. Initially, budgets should be prepared in two forms. One form should detail income and expenditures by line item (e.g., acquisitions, equipment, and salaries) for the library as a whole and for each operating unit. The second budget form should aggregate direct and indirect costs by major program area regardless of operating responsibilities; for example, this budget should estimate such program costs as the following:

- Total collection development and preservation costs, including estimated costs of such factors as:
    - Acquisitions, replacements, bindings and repairs, and duplications
    - Resources and other staff time spent on collection development and acquisitions
    - Materials and records processing and other support unit activities
    - Prorated operating costs of stack space used for shelving materials

—Capital improvement projects designed for preservation and
maintenance
- Collection development and preservation costs in terms of:
—Cataloged volumes, serials, special documents, microfilm,
and other media
—Major subject and academic areas (humanistic and historical,
science, medical science, law, etc.)
- Costs of resource and other services provided to users, including
cost aggregates of categories such as:
—Information and referral, including general orientation, student advisory, use of catalog, and ready reference services
—In-depth subject reference and research assistance
—Instructional assistance (including reserve collections and
staff, classroom lectures and presentations, time for special
bibliographies, etc.)

The Assistant University Librarian for Planning should be responsible for developing a program approach along the above lines for
implementation throughout the system. He should hold a series
of meetings with library officials and staff members to explain the
approach and to begin setting guidelines for defining programs and
associated costs. Sample program budgets should first be developed
in a single program area and then tested. The libraries should formally
seek counsel and advice from faculty members versed in program
budget techniques.

It is important that the purpose of program budgets be kept in
mind as costs are distributed among the defined program areas.
A program budget is an improved tool for decision making that
provides comparative costs and performance information. Thus,
the costs that are aggregated in a given program should be exclusively
attributable to that program.

APPROACHES TO LEADERSHIP AND
SUPERVISION

Columbia's libraries should adopt approaches to leadership and
supervision which are oriented to the achievement of objectives

and high staff productivity. Responsibility for leadership should be clearly assigned.

Roles of Managerial and Supervisory Staff

Individuals in managerial and supervisory roles in Columbia's libraries frequently interpret their responsibilities simply as maintaining administrative discipline and order. Too often the leadership opportunities which these individuals have in terms of mobilizing and developing library staff resources are not recognized or acted upon.

In the future, Columbia's libraries should stress the staff development potential of leadership positions. In particular, managerial and supervisory personnel should employ standard practices of good management: delegation of authority, establishment and maintenance of clear reporting relationships, and involvement of their staff in planning and decision making. Compensation for equivalent positions should be comparable. Managerial and supervisory personnel should actively concern themselves with the career growth of their staff members. They should participate actively in formulating development plans and should periodically evaluate individual performance. They should constantly strive to provide staff members with opportunities to test and develop their potential.

The Vice President and University Librarian is responsible for providing overall leadership to Columbia's libraries. One of his major efforts should be to see that high standards of leadership and supervision are maintained throughout the system. He should make certain that the Associate and Assistant University Librarians know what is expected of them and hold them to high standards of performance, counseling them individually to strengthen their leadership and supervisory effectiveness.

All managerial and supervisory personnel should be given detailed responsibilities for leadership and supervision. They should be expected to perform effectively, and their performance in these areas should be evaluated periodically and strengthened through counseling and guidance. To move toward this expanded leadership role for middle management and top administrative personnel, several developments are necessary. The libraries should:

- Commit time and money to supervisory training and managerial development activities that provide opportunities for librarians to learn and utilize sound management principles. All beginning supervisors, for example, should be required to complete a training course and complete a directed reading program.
- Establish criteria for evaluating supervisors in terms of leadership performance.
- Pursue an assessment and promotion approach that identifies potential leaders.
- Establish a library management intern plan to secure recent graduates and provide intensive experience.

Staff Motivation

Supervisors at Columbia's libraries often limit subordinates to prescribed duties, a practice which maximizes control but impedes the full exercise of staff potential and reduces motivation. Motivation is the key to successful supervision. Leaders should stress practices and policies that reinforce motivations supportive of library objectives. A number of common-sense approaches have been successful in other institutions and should be adopted by the libraries' managerial and supervisory personnel.

Managerial and supervisory personnel should evince confidence and trust in their subordinates. They should be supportive of their staff members. Immediate supervisors should obtain and use subordinates' ideas and opinions to a greater extent than appears to be the case at present. Subordinates, in turn, should have confidence and trust in their supervisors and feel free to discuss work-related matters with them. Such practices and policies result not only in improved staff identity with the goals of the organization, but also—through better decision-making—in improved performance. To move towards these mutually supportive relationships that can improve both motivation and performance, adequate training should be given all supervisory staff to increase their understanding and awareness of leadership dynamics.

Staff Planning and Decision Making

The ability to bring together the skills and resources needed for informed decision making is an essential ingredient in an efficiently run enterprise. Managerial and supervisory personnel at Columbia's libraries should pursue this approach wherever possible in the units and groups for which they are responsible. Immediate priority in implementing the recommended plan of organization should be given to designating appropriate committees, task forces, and program and technical advisory groups, as suggested in Chapter II.

Leadership Training Opportunities and Programs

Individuals assigned managerial or supervisory responsibilities should be given opportunities for management training within the libraries or elsewhere. The Personnel Office should itself develop, or seek within the university, training opportunities that can be offered staff members periodically. Seminars and group sessions are effective means that can be readily developed to consider particular aspects of management and personnel practices. Sessions offering orientation to resource, service, and support programs should be provided for newer employees who are seeking executive-level careers. Other topics such as planning and staff training techniques should be emphasized.

WORKING RELATIONSHIPS AND
COMMUNICATION

Meaningful working relationships and open communication throughout Columbia's libraries are essential for the recommended organization and staffing plans to work effectively. Communication is particularly important because of the operations of a number of groups, the complexities of multiple reporting relationships, and the organization coverage of the resources units.

Although improved recently through the use of committees, staff meetings, and memoranda, present patterns of working relationships and communication in Columbia's libraries are inadequate for several reasons.

- Staff and operating units have tended to operate in isolation from one another.
- Attitudes have tended to be narrowly focused on the individual unit rather than on the achievement of overall library goals.
- Effective means have not been found to achieve meaningful identity.
- Operating staff members have tended to distrust management decisions in which they have not participated.
- Administrative structure has sometimes precluded staff members from developing functional relationships that could enhance overall performance.

Recommended management and professional practices, coupled with the proposed organization and staffing plans, should foster communication and working relationships that will facilitate the achievement of overall library objectives in a cooperative and supportive manner.

Top Management Working Relationships
and Communication

The plan of organization proposed for the future should be used to make working relationships and communication effective at all levels. As suggested in Chapter II, the Vice President and University Librarian should provide overall executive direction and professional leadership to Columbia's libraries. He and the heads of the five major units should share the same library philosophies and objectives and should work together as a "professional partnership." Confidence and communication among them should be extremely high. This top management team should meet at least once a week and there should be almost daily communication between the Vice President and University Librarian and each of the other top executives.

Similar working relationships and meeting and communication patterns should prevail within and between the operating units of the library system. Unit heads should be responsible for seeing that this is so within their units. Inter-unit communication and comunication between the libraries and the faculty should be fostered by the work of committees, task forces, and advisory groups as well as through direct day-to-day work. For example, an arts council might be established to facilitate communication among staff members concerned with collections and services in this area.

Communication Throughout the System

Significant improvements have been made in communication by the use of the Director's newsletter, staff meetings, and distribution of committee minutes. There is a general feeling, however, based on the interviews conducted and the results of the Likert profile, that more is needed—not only more of the same type of communication, but also greater sophistication in methods. Too much reliance is placed on informal word-of-mouth contacts for information, particularly in relation to position openings, career opportunities, and policy developments.

A major amount of interaction and communication should be directed toward achieving the libraries' objectives, on both an individual and a group basis. Communication should flow upward, downward, and among peers. Present methods emphasize downward flow of information at the expense of lateral or upward flow. The Representative Committee of Librarians is increasingly viewed as a communications link between the central administration and staff librarians.

Downward communication should be initiated at all levels. Senior staff members should seek to give subordinates all relevant information that they need and desire. Junior staff members should also feel responsible for initiating upward communication, usually following lines of organization. Lateral communication among colleagues should be free and accurate, unhindered by feelings of competition or hostility.

Staff Meetings

Staff meetings are gaining popularity although several major operating units (e.g., cataloging) do not meet formally as a group to discuss mutual problems or exchange information. The practice of holding staff meetings should be expanded, with schedules and agenda prepared for larger groups and with full participation of individual staff members. Library staff members should recognize their responsibility to communicate freely, informally, and directly with one another and with faculty members, students, and others.

The present practice of holding regular meetings of the entire professional staff should continue and the Vice President and University Librarian should preside. These meetings serve as an important system-wide forum for reviewing and discussing policy and program matters. Accordingly, regular presentations should be made by each major operating unit concerning developments so that ideas and information are shared. The Vice President and University Librarian should also use this forum for explaining major decisions and why and how they were reached.

Regular staff meetings should also be held within library units. Meetings should have agenda to ensure that important topics are covered and a record of proceedings is maintained. Sessions should be conducted to encourage participation, to raise points of interest or concern, and to facilitate discussions.

Formal and Informal Communication

Written material is often not available to lower-level staff members at Columbia's libraries. Supervisors sometimes neglect to distribute documentation directly applicable to daily operations. Operating unit bulletin boards and a standardized routing system may solve this problem. Memoranda should also be used freely by library staff members at all levels, and copies should be provided as standard practice to appropriate staff members interested in the topic covered.

Annual and other formal reports are presently prepared for the library system as a whole and for each major unit. These should be redesigned and standardized to inform recipients about objectives, goals, program progress and problems, financial results, and performance.

Committee, task force, and advisory group minutes should be carefully prepared and circulated soon after each meeting. Standard formats should be used and minutes should identify continuing topics to be discussed at future meetings. Minutes should be available to interested staff and faculty members. The accomplishments of committees should be summarized semiannually.

Training in Communication Techniques

Staff members at Columbia's libraries often find group dynamics unfamiliar and disconcerting. As a result, the potential contributions of collective efforts are often not realized. Training in effective oral communication should be provided to staff members who have frequent contact with library users. Committee and working group chairmen should be trained in committee procedures, such as agenda preparation, rules of order, leading discussions, and group dynamics. Guidance should also be available in manuals on communication techniques.

STAFF DEVELOPMENT

The continuing development of present staff capabilities is vital to the libraries' future success. Effective staff development depends upon (1) accurate position descriptions and (2) training and recruitment programs to acquire people qualified to fill these positions.

Overall Approach

Columbia's libraries should adopt a formal staff development plan designed to help meet their organization and staffing requirements and to assist staff members in achieving their career objectives. In the past, little staff development effort has been undertaken on a systemwide coordinated basis, although occasional programs such as the Cornell Industrial Relations Seminar have been used to deal with immediate and specific problems.

For the future, the library system's staff development approach should be comprehensive. Plans should include all categories of library staff (executive, librarian, specialist, and clerical) and encompass all library units. In addition, the approach should be carefully related to Columbia's personnel and other plans.

Elements of the Plan

At present, aside from clerical classification schemes, no staff development plans exist that are adequate for effective individual planning and growth. The libraries should now prepare development plans for executive, librarian, and specialist personnel. The plan for each category should include each of the following areas of concern:

- *Staff Needs*—These should include (1) projections of staff requirements by staff category, class, and position title and (2) estimates of availability of needed staff at Columbia's libraries and those that will need to be recruited elsewhere.
- *Career Development Approach*—This should identify the career progression steps and requirements in the service, resource, administrative, executive, and other areas. It should indicate preparatory or on-the-job training needed and identify the training which the libraries, university faculties, or others should provide. It should identify the scope of and approach to individual staff development plans which should be formulated and executed for each staff member. Procedures and schedules for staff evaluations should be spelled out in terms of performance, progress against development plan, etc., and should include how and by whom the review will be carried out.
- *Managerial and Supervisory Responsibilities*—These should specify orientation, on-the-job training, and other training responsibilities of managerial and supervisory staff, as well as outlines of training programs and resources.

The overall plan should be reviewed and adopted by the Vice President and University Librarian and his cabinet. Individual unit heads, working closely with the Personnel Office, will be responsible for applying the plan to their own circumstances.

Involvement in Planning

Staff development should be a top-management responsibility in Columbia's libraries. The Vice President and University Librarian should guide the formulation of development plans and approve them. The Assistant University Librarian for Personnel should be the officer principally responsibile for designing and implementing these plans.

Library staff members should be involved formally (i.e., through committees, task forces, and advisory groups) and informally in the formulation of staff development plans. Librarians should participate in the development of all plans. Specialist and clerical staff members should be involved in the preparation of plans for their own groups. Appropriate university officials in personnel should also review and approve library staff development plans.

Individual Development Plans

Highly individualized plans should be prepared for each member of Columbia's library staff. Each plan should be prepared in accordance with overall library plans by the individual with his immediate supervisor. The Associate and Assistant University Librarians should review the plans of professional staff members in their units and should forward them to the Assistant University Librarian for Personnel for his review and approval and for filing. Each plan should be formalized and well documented. Information about each plan should be freely available to the staff members covered by the plan.

The plan should specify specific development steps that each staff member should take to further his performance and career goals. The steps should be designed to enhance professional capabilities and work effectiveness through formal and informal training, reading, and other similar techniques.

Staff members should be helped and encouraged to define their career interests, particularly as Columbia's libraries have sufficiently varied opportunities to satisfy most individual goals without forcing talented staff to look elsewhere. Also, the process of defining career objectives should benefit the system by building a more dynamic staff interested in seeking expanded or refined levels of challenge.

An ongoing staff development process often implies an "up or out" professional growth approach; management experience amply documents the correlation between job challenge and performance.

In many organizations, however, the greater challenges and rewards are available only by climbing the administrative ladder. The proposed plan of staffing for Columbia's libraries, while appropriately rewarding administrative responsibility, sets professional competence—demonstrated and enhanced through individual initiative—as the central criterion for a successful career.

Periodic Reviews

Performance reviews are presently conducted for beginning professional staff at Columbia's libraries. The format and the involvement of staff are left to the immediate supervisor, however, and no guidelines are provided on the content or objectives of the review process. In fact, most junior staff members have not had the opportunity to discuss with their supervisors the nature of their contribution or where improvement is needed.

The supervisor who knows the individual's work should conduct the review process. In addition, other professional staff members should participate in the review process in cases where multiple reporting relationships exist. The Assistant University Librarian for Personnel, or someone designated in his office, should be actively involved in the review process.

Uniform policies concerning the nature and frequency of staff evaluation should be established to assure equitable treatment of all staff members. Individuals should be given reasonable time between evaluations to demonstrate accomplishment. Spacing should also take into account the sensitivity and level of the position and the seniority of the individual involved. Thus, a new employee should be evaluated after his first six months of provisional employment and then immediately after his first year. A policy of annual evaluation should be adopted for all professional staff members, except for those who have reached the upper grades in their positions and are unlikely to advance to higher levels of responsibility. In these instances, reviews of a formal nature may be two or three years apart and compensation adjustments should reflect increased experience and refined skills.

Staff Development Committee

Professional staff evaluations should be made by the Staff Development Committee. The Assistant University Librarian for Personnel should schedule and coordinate the activities of the committee and the roster of individuals to be reviewed. The committee should collect information on the full range of professional activities of the individual being reviewed and recommend appropriate salary and other actions to be taken based on its evaluation. The Vice President and University Librarian should rely to a great extent on these recommendations; however, he is the final authority concerning action taken.

The committee's evaluation should consider both the individual's performance of currently assigned responsibilities and his progress in terms of long-term professional growth and career development. To be meaningful, evaluations should be made against valid position descriptions and career development plans. The Personnel Office should prepare, with the advice and counsel of the Staff Development Committee, a list of criteria to be used for evaluation. These criteria should encompass several areas and may vary according to the position so that evaluation can be approximately geared to the individual's level of competence and experience.

Performance of current position responsibilities should include an overall assessment of the incumbent's understanding of the position and its duties, level of accomplishment in performing specific duties, and ability to function professionally without constant supervision. This criterion should extend to his judgment in reaching decisions and referring problems upward (and downward), organization and use of time, follow-through, effectiveness in working with others, ability to write and speak effectively, and administrative competence in preparing and executing plans and budgets.

It should also include, where appropriate, an assessment of his effectiveness as a supervisor in delegating authority and assigning responsibility, involving staff in formulating plans, and overall performance of the unit in terms of, e.g., staff turnover, absenteeism, morale, progress against plans and budgets, and level of satisfaction of those being served. An assessment of his ability to help individual staff members to develop and improve performance, his demonstrated capacity to motivate staff members towards accomplishment of unit and library objectives, and his effectiveness in communicating policies and procedures throughout the unit should also be made. The degree to which the unit's operations are in keeping with overall objectives and plans and the supervisor's accountability in terms of accuracy and timeliness of reporting should also be appraised.

Progress in professional growth and development is an important area for evaluation of the adequacy of academic training in terms of career goals, professional motivations and attitudes, and level of professional accomplishment in terms of career goals. It should include an appraisal of professional activities such as active memberships, attendance at seminars, and continuing education. Participation in and contribution to committees and task forces and the compatibility of his demonstrated strengths and weaknesses with stated career goals should also be part of the appraisal.

In order for the evaluation to be accurate and as balanced as possible, it should be based on information gained from several sources. The immediate supervisor should, of course, be a prime source of information in evaluating performance as well as professional growth. Professionals with whom ongoing working relationships have been established or who have shared committee responsibilities with the individual should also be asked for their evaluation, as appropriate. In addition, faculty and student representatives who know the individual and can offer a wider perspective should be contacted for their appraisal. These inputs, together with administrative records of attendance, publications, and past reviews, should constitute the basis for the committee's overall findings.

Evaluations should be expressed in standard format in a written statement that synthesizes the committee's findings, conclusions, and recommendations. The statement should be based on advance work by a subcommittee assigned to collect pertinent data and to formulate the preliminary appraisal. Subcommittees will be essential to enable the committee to evaluate effectively 150 professional staff members in Columbia's library system each year. The subcommittee should personally interview those knowledgeable about the individual's performance and professional growth and submit its written draft appraisal to the full committee in advance of the meeting.

While subcommittees have a vital role in the evaluation process, the final review statement should be approved by the full committee. In this context, it is important to understand that the committee's function is not to evaluate an individual based on its own collective understanding and opinions, except as developed from the concrete evidence presented. Its key function is to discern from those who know the individual the essentials of his demonstrated achievements and long-term potential. Thus, the committee should sift through available information to evaluate strengths and weaknesses objectively and to recommend steps the individual should take to strengthen performance and enhance career progress.

The eligibility of an individual for position assignment, reassignment, promotion, or termination should be decided by considering review findings. Change in compensation should also be based on the outcome of the performance review.

It is recognized that the personnel appraisal approach may be difficult for many staff to accept who have for so many years been without regular development reviews. Thus implementation may need to be phased to ease into the process gradually to gain acceptance of the concept. Consideration of salary matters by a committee may be a particularly sensitive issue and initially, perhaps, the focus of the committee review should be solely on professional development opportunities.

This chapter has proposed management approaches that should be employed for the new organization and staffing plans to be effective. The next and final chapter of the report suggests an approach that should be taken to implement the recommendations in this report.

CHAPTER FIVE

Implementation Approach

Implementing recommendations requiring the magnitude of change proposed for Columbia's libraries will be complex and difficult. Careful planning and preparation will be required at every step. Because of the importance of staff understanding certain basic management principles that underlie many of the recommendations, orientation and training will need to be provided as part of the implementation process. Worthy proposals have failed elsewhere because of poor preparation and planning.

This chapter sets forth an approach to help the libraries implement the recommendations of this report. It suggests integrated steps that should be taken in sequence to (1) acquaint university officials and library staff with change and prepare them for it and (2) implement change in an orderly fashion. The approach set forth in this chapter is a tentative one that will need to be carefully reviewed and revised by the staff of Columbia's libraries to make it theirs. Review and updating should be continuous in order to refine plans in light of experience gained as implementation proceeds.

PRESENTATION AND REVIEW OF PROPOSALS

As a first step, the proposals should be carefully presented to library staff and reviewed and approved by appropriate university officials.

160

Acceptance in principle of the proposed new structures by the President and the Executive Vice President for Academic Affairs and Provost will be a necessary initial requirement for the libraries to be able to pursue implementation actively with the full support of university officials. Some recommendations may require action by the Board of Trustees to change existing university statutes. In addition, key faculty and student groups will need to be informed.

Accordingly, the libraries should take several steps to build university understanding and acceptance of the proposals:

- The Director of Libraries should prepare a brief five- to ten-page paper for submission to the President and other university officials (1) explaining the changes desired and their benefits and (2) setting forth implications of the changes for the statutes, existing policies, and other matters requiring formal attention. The purpose of this paper should be to obtain approval in principle from appropriate university officials so that the libraries' Director and staff can proceed with implementation.
- A meeting should be held with the President and the Executive Vice Presidents, and other administrative officers as appropriate, to discuss and clarify the proposals and achieve broad consensus that the change appears desirable.
- Following approval by top university officials, the Director of Libraries should send a similar brief summary letter to the University Senate Library Committee and should meet subsequently with the committee to answer questions.
- Publication of an article explaining the reasons for and objectives of the change should be sought in *The Spectator*, Columbia's student newspaper.
- A list should be drawn up of key faculty members and groups which should be informed of intended changes, and specific approaches adopted for so doing.

The way in which presentations about the changes are made to the university community will have a bearing on the expectations generated about how soon benefits will result. It is clear, however, that the magnitude of change proposed will take time before optimum staffing and organization plans are operative. Therefore, as a strategy, the libraries should maintain a relatively low profile vis-à-vis the general university community until initial implementation has been achieved. This posture will allow change to occur in an orderly fashion, while minimizing the possibilities of premature demands being made on the system.

Once appropriate university officials have approved the proposed plan in principle, steps should be taken to summarize the recommendations for the library staff. The purpose of this process should be to (1) build staff understanding and acceptance and (2) gain staff inputs to help refine the proposals. Before involving the entire staff, the Director of Libraries and his key executives and staff should be publicly committed to the need for change along the broad lines of the report. Introducing the report in a positive context is important at least to alleviate resistance to change and to focus energies on more constructive concerns of making the plan work. At the same time, maintaining a position of listening to staff viewpoints will be important for library leaders to be confident that all opinions and concerns are taken into account in the final plan.

Staff members must be involved in both hearing about the plan and implementing it. While other comments concerning the role of staff members are made elsewhere in this report, the initial concern is that staff members be well informed. Accordingly, the proposals should be explained systematically throughout the libraries along such lines as the following:

- The Director of Libraries should present the plan to key staff members from operating units and his own office. These staff members should be given the summary statement prepared for the university administration and have access to copies of the final report. At least two meetings close together should be held so that questions can be answered more fully and an approach to the staff developed and agreed upon.
- Staff members are likely to be apprehensive about how their personal situations might fare through the change; such anxiety, if permitted to develop, could have widespread negative effects on library performance. It is essential, therefore, that the Director of Libraries stress to unit heads and other key individuals the need for unified executive support for the plan in their contacts with other staff members.

- Shortly following the meetings of key unit heads, a meeting of the full professional staff should be held to present the plan. Simultaneously, appropriate measures should be taken to inform nonprofessional staff. The Director of Libraries should preside and, in addition to highlighting the proposed changes, should indicate the proposed plan for meeting with staff for clarification and discussion purposes thereafter. He should also outline the broad strategy and goals of implementation.

- Subsequently, unit heads should meet with their managerial and supervisory staff members to go over the plan and to begin discussing implications for their respective units. At these and other such meetings, it will be important that, in addition to general discussion, sufficient time be devoted at the end to the specific steps that should be taken next, such as appointment of implementation groups, selection of cabinet officials, and so on.

Once these initial presentations are made and there is general acceptance of the plan among university officials and library staff, implementation will be well under way.

DESIGNATION OF PRINCIPAL OFFICERS
RESPONSIBLE FOR IMPLEMENTATION

A fundamental implementation step should be appointment by the Vice President and University Librarian of the three Associate University Librarians (Resources, Services, and Support) and the two Assistant University Librarians (Personnel and Planning). These top people should be appointed before other organization and staffing changes are made so they can work together to develop a mutually satisfactory plan for implementation. Even after these cabinet people are appointed, the present lines of authority and responsibility should continue to be observed until formal organization change is achieved. Thus, most of the day-to-day operations of the libraries would continue to be administered as at present. The two individuals appointed to the planning and personnel positions, however, should immediately assume their responsibilities because of the comparatively few staff members in their units. The newly appointed cabinet should help the Vice President and University Librarian to plan and then carry through an orderly transition with as little disruption of library services as possible.

It is useful to highlight the characteristics the individuals filling the top positions in resources, services, and support should have. The Associate University Librarian for Resources should be a respected scholar-librarian capable of mobilizing the subject-resource librarian skills to develop collections and provide in-depth instruction and research services across a number of disciplines. He should also be able to relate well to the academic community and be responsive to their intellectual interests. The role of the Associate University Librarian for Services is also critical and in some ways more demanding. He should have a clear professional commitment to making the libraries as efficient and easy to use as possible and a capacity for managing large numbers of people and complex library operations. The Associate University Librarian for Support should also possess strong management skills and be highly performance oriented. He should possess a working knowledge of business services and management techniques, as well as be familiar with complex materials processing requirements.

The appointment of these individuals should be based on well-thought-out position descriptions that communicate the essentials and differences of each job.

FORMULATION AND ADOPTION
OF A DETAILED PLAN FOR
IMPLEMENTATION

A detailed plan of integrated steps should be developed and adopted by the top executive staff to guide each phase of implementation. An illustrative plan of action that can serve as an initial implementation guide useful for monitoring progress is provided in Exhibit 43, on page 166. The Vice President and University Librarian and his cabinet should review and formally adopt the plan after it has been modified as needed. In turn, each Associate and Assistant

University Librarian should develop work plans to be followed within his respective area to be sure targets in the overall plan can be achieved.

Once adopted, the plan for implementation should be circulated among key executive and supervisory staff. As implementation begins, the Vice President and University Librarian and his cabinet should meet at least weekly to evaluate progress and to modify the plan of action as needed to keep steps in phase. The Vice President and University Librarian should make reports on progress periodically to the professional staff meetings and via his newsletter. A realistic plan of action and regular reporting on progress should help preserve a sense of order and achievement as changes are made.

IMPLEMENTATION AND THE PLANNING OFFICE

The Assistant University Librarian for Planning should be designated the principal staff person helping the Vice President and University Librarian guide and coordinate the implementation process. His function in implementation should be comparable to what happens during the budgeting process. He should establish target dates and schedules, monitor progress, and schedule the many individual efforts that should proceed apace for the process to be effective. The planning officer should maintain the master plan of action to which the Vice President and University Librarian can turn for an immediate assessment of where things stand. The planning officer should also coordinate meetings, establish formal turnover dates for organization and staffing changes to be made, and assemble unit descriptions and policy statements in appropriate manuals and files. Communication will be a critical function for the Planning Office. It should have staff responsibility for helping uncover critical issues where several library viewpoints are involved and for resolving issues by bringing appropriate staff together.

EXHIBIT 43 (1)

Columbia University

PLAN OF ACTION

Recommendation	Action To Be Taken
. Inform officials and staff and gain needed approval to proceed with implementation	. Adopt report in principle
	. Present broad changes desired to university officials for approval to proceed
	. Acquaint University Senate Library Committee and selected faculty and students with proposed changes

	. Inform library staff of proposed organization and staffing changes
	  - Meet with division heads
	  - Meet with full professional staff
	  - Meet with unit supervisory and other staff

. Develop top management team to plan for and guide implementation	. Appoint Associate and Assistant University Librarians - Prepare top executive position descriptions

. Adopt plan of action to guide implementation	. Review, modify, and approve overall plan of action for the libraries
	  - Prepare individual work unit plans
	  - Review overall plan of action by key staff
	  - Highlight plan of action schedule to professional staff

. Assign responsibility to coordinate implementation	. Designate Assistant University Librarian for Planning as chief staff coordinator of implementation

. Establish needed overall committees
  - Professional Advisory Committee
  - Staff Development Committee
	. Draw up panel list of eligible personnel to serve on these committees

	. Appoint committee members
. Establish groups to help guide implementation	. Designate Professional Advisory Committee as chief implementation advisory group and suggest sub-organization as needed
	. Designate Staff Development Committee as implementation group concerning personnel matters and staffing

By Whom	Completion Date
. Vice President and University Librarian and his top staff	. February 1972
. Vice President and University Librarian	. February 1972
. President and the Executive Vice President for Academic Affairs and Provost	
. Vice President and University Librarian and the division heads	. February 1972
. Vice President and University Librarian and the executive staff	. February 1972
. Vice President and University Librarian	. February 1972
. Vice President and University Librarian	. February 1972
. Division and unit heads	. February 1972 on
. Vice President and University Librarian	. February-April 1972
. Vice President and University Librarian and Personnel Office	. February 1972
. Vice President and University Librarian and the Associate and Assistant University Librarians	. February-April 1972
. Associate and Assistant University Librarians	. March-May 1972
. Executive and supervisory staff	. March-May 1972
. Vice President and University Librarian	. February-March 1972
. Vice President and University Librarian	. February-April 1972
. Representative Committee of Librarians	. February-March 1972
. Vice President and University Librarian	. March 1972
. Vice President and University Librarian	. March 1972
. Vice President and University Librarian	. March 1972

EXHIBIT 43 (2)

Recommendation	Action To Be Taken
	. Designate Representative Committee of Librarians as having broad review and comment role concerning all major implementation plans developed
	. Designate other special advisory implementation groups as needed
. Improve management capabilities through training of executives and staff	
. The Director of Libraries should be given the title of Vice President and University Librarian	. Propose title change to the President for approval and to modify existing statutes as needed

. Revise administrative plan of organization providing for:
  - Services Group
  - Resources Group
  - Support Group
  - Planning Office
  - Personnel Office
  - Distinctive collections, Law Library Center, and Medical Science Information Center
	. Review and adopt administrative plan proposed in Booz, Allen & Hamilton report
	  - Prepare unit descriptions
	  - Review overall plan

	. Establish July target date for revised plan of organization to become operational
	. Establish internal plans of organization for each group and office and for distinctive collections, the Law Library Center, and the Medical Science Information Center
	. Appoint individuals to be responsible for each unit under the proposed plan of organization
	. Review unit objectives, programs, and internal organization and staffing structures with appointed unit heads

. Develop policy manual to guide initial implementation and continuing operations	. Prepare, review, and adopt policy statements concerning user privileges; interlibrary loans; relations with university officials, faculty, and student groups; functional responsibilities in the organization; lines of reporting and working relationships; staff development; others
	  - For all libraries
	  - For each group and office

	. Assign the Assistant University Librarian for Planning responsibility for maintaining central policy manual and coordinating efforts to keep it up to date

By Whom	Completion Date
. Vice President and University Librarian	. March 1972
. Vice President and University Librarian and his top cabinet	. March 1972 on
. Vice President and University Librarian . President . Board of Trustees	. January-February 1972
. Vice President and University Librarian and his top cabinet	. February-May 1972
. Vice President and University Librarian with his top cabinet . Implementation groups	. February-March 1972 . March-May 1972
. Vice President and University Librarian	. May 1972
. Vice President and University Librarian . Associate and Assistant University Librarians	. March-June 1972
. Respective Associate and Assistant University Librarians with approval of the Vice President and University Librarian	. April-May 1972
. Respective Associate and Assistant University Librarians . Unit heads . Implementation groups	. May-June 1972
. Vice President and University Librarian . Associate and Assistant University Librarians . Implementation groups . President and the Executive Vice President for Academic Affairs and Provost (concerning broad library policies affecting the academic community)	. April-June 1972
. Vice President and University Librarian	. April 1972

EXHIBIT 43 (3)

Recommendation	Action To Be Taken

. Establish a Services Group to operate subject centers and provide first- and second-line library services	. Designate three subject centers and their allied libraries:
	  - Humanistic and Historical Studies Center
	  - Social Science Center
	  - Science Information Center
	
	. Designate organization units and titles within each subject center:
	  - Access Services Department
	  - Instructional Materials and Services Department
	  - Allied libraries
	
	. Appoint individuals to be responsible for subject centers and individual units; review unit descriptions, staffing patterns, working relationships, and other matters with them
	
	. Formulate and approve statements of programs to be offered by each subject center and in each Instructional Materials and Services Department and Access Services Department
	
	. Assign staff to fill positions in Services Group
	
	Define tentative position descriptions for key staff

. Establish a Resources Group responsible for collection development, in-depth reference and research assistance, classroom instruction, and original cataloging	. Designate organization units and titles within the Resources Group:
	  - Resource Development and Utilization Division
	  - Bibliographic Control Division
	
	. Appoint individuals to be responsible for divisions and for major subject areas within each division
	
	. Formulate and approve statements of resources programs to be offered by each division in conjunction with each subject center and centrally
	
	. Assign staff to fill positions in Resources Group
	
	. Define tentative position descriptions for key staff

By Whom	Completion Date
. Vice President and University Librarian . Associate University Librarian for Services	. March-April 1972
. Associate University Librarian for Services	. March-April 1972
. Associate University Librarian for Services and the Vice President and University Librarian	. April-May 1972
. Associate University Librarian for Services . Directors of subject centers . Department heads . Implementation groups	. May-June 1972
. Associate University Librarian for Services	. July 1972
. Directors of subject centers . Department heads . Personnel Office	. May-June 1972
. Vice President and University Librarian . Associate University Librarian for Resources	. March-April 1972
. Associate University Librarian for Resources and the Vice President and University Librarian	. April-May 1972
. Associate University Librarian for Resources . Division and department heads . Implementation groups	. May-June 1972
. Associate University Librarian for Resources	. July 1972
. Division and department heads . Personnel Office	. May-June 1972

EXHIBIT 43 (4)

Recommendation	Action To Be Taken
. Establish a Support Group to provide essential business, analysis, and record production services for all Columbia libraries	. Designate organization units and titles within the Support Group: - Records and Materials Processing Department - Business Services Department - Library Research and Analysis Department . Appoint individuals to be responsible for departments . Formulate and approve statements of support programs to be conducted by each support department, with initial guides to measure performance . Assign staff to fill positions in Support Group . Define tentative position descriptions for key staff
. Establish distinctive collections, Law Library Center, and Medical Science Information Center responsible to the Vice President and University Librarian	. Designate organization units, titles, and unit descriptions for: - Law Library Center - Medical Science Information Center - Manuscripts and Rare Books Collections - Architecture Collections - East Asian Collections - University Archival Collections . Appoint individuals to be responsible for these special libraries . Assign staff to fill positions in the special libraries and define tentative position descriptions for key staff
. Establish the Personnel Office responsible for manpower planning, recruiting and development, training programs, union liaison, and other aspects of personnel administration	. Adopt plan of staff organization for the Personnel Office and define responsibilities of each unit . Assign staff members in unit and become operational immediately
. Establish the Planning Office responsible for developing, coordinating, and monitoring library planning efforts	. Adopt plan of staff organization for the Planning Office and define responsibilities of each unit . Assign staff members in unit and become operational immediately

By Whom	Completion Date
. Vice President and University Librarian . Associate University Librarian for Support	. March-April 1972
. Associate University Librarian for Support and the Vice President and University Librarian	. April-May 1972
. Associate University Librarian for Support . Department heads . Implementation groups	. May-June 1972
. Associate University Librarian for Support	. July 1972
. Department heads . Personnel Office	. May-June 1972
. Vice President and University Librarian	. March-April 1972
. Vice President and University Librarian	. April-May 1972
. Directors of special libraries and the Vice President and University Librarian	. July 1972
. Assistant University Librarian for Personnel and the Vice President and University Librarian	. March 1972
. Assistant University Librarian for Personnel	. March-April 1972
. Assistant University Librarian for Planning and the Vice President and University Librarian	. March 1972
. Assistant University Librarian for Planning	. March-April 1972

EXHIBIT 43 (5)

Recommendation	Action To Be Taken

. Create appropriate program and technical advisory committees to promote the close working relationships needed within and among the several groups and offices	. Identify library program and functional areas where advisory groups should be established to meet periodically to discuss problems of improving quality and coordination of services:
	  - Within respective groups
	  - Interorganizational committees for functional-subject areas
	
	. Define the scope of advisory committee responsibilities, composition, and frequency of meetings once proposed plan of organization becomes operational
	
	. Appoint staff to fill advisory committees after proposed plan becomes operational

. Adopt and implement a revised personnel classification plan providing for:
  - Executive positions
  - Librarian positions
  - Specialist positions
  - Clerical positions
	. Assign Assistant University Librarian for Personnel primary responsibility for staff review of plan and for coordinating a process for top management and implementation group review of proposed plan
	
	. Review, modify, and adopt Booz, Allen & Hamilton classification plan as initial framework for implementation of staffing plans within the proposed organization units
	
	. Work with top management team in developing unit staffing plans and key staff position descriptions to be compatible with overall classification plan
	
	. Establish a year-long schedule for development, review, and modification of position descriptions throughout the libraries based on (1) the overall classification plan and (2) actual work experience as the new organization is operational
	  - Indicate group and unit responsibilities
	  - Indicate committee responsibilities
	
	. Carry out and complete year-long plan to produce accurate position descriptions in accordance with classification plan

By Whom	Completion Date
. Vice President and University Librarian and the Associate and Assistant University Librarians	. April-May 1972
. Vice President and University Librarian and the Associate and Assistant University Librarians	. June-July 1972
. Vice President and University Librarian and the Associate and Assistant University Librarians	. August-September 1972
. Vice President and University Librarian	. March 1972
. Vice President and University Librarian and the Associate and Assistant University Librarians	. March-June 1972
. Implementation groups, including the Representative Committee of Librarians and the Staff Development and Professional Advisory Committees	. April-June 1972
. Assistant University Librarian for Personnel	. May-July 1972
. Assistant University Librarian for Personnel	. July-August 1972
. Vice President and University Librarian and top management group	. September 1972-August 1973

EXHIBIT 43 (6)

Recommendation	Action To Be Taken
. Adopt and implement a staffing plan for the assignment of staff among proposed organization units	. Conduct and analyze an interest survey of present staff to determine where individuals are qualified and would prefer to work and develop in the proposed plan of organization; indicate that not all requests for changes will be able to be approved until actual experience with new organization is gained
	. Convey survey results to top management group to consider in working out initial staff plans for implementation
	. Review and consolidate staff rosters by new organization unit that will go into effect when proposed plans become operational in July 1972
	. Notify and discuss with individual staff members proposed assignments under the new plan of organization, including responsibilities, reporting relationships, etc.
. Establish and fill specialist positions to perform specialized responsibilities not requiring the skills of a professionally trained librarian	. Identify throughout the plan of organization the positions to be filled by specialists over the short and long term
	. Determine which positions can be filled by specialists as of July, and conduct orientation and training programs to gear selected individuals for these positions
	. Establish goals for developing and assigning specialists to positions over the next year and for recruitment and training programs
. Give high priority to development of the libraries' human resources	. Prepare, adopt, and distribute policy statements concerning the need to place greater emphasis on developing staff capabilities to deliver the quality of services desired, notifying all managerial and supervisory staff of their primary responsibility in this area
. Utilize group problem-solving approaches wherever appropriate to maximize the utilization of needed staff resources	. Develop training programs to be provided by non-library staff (unless the capability is available) for managerial and supervisory staff

By Whom	Completion Date
. Assistant University Librarian for Personnel	. February-March 1972
. Assistant University Librarian for Personnel . Associate and Assistant University Librarians	. March-May 1972
. Assistant University Librarian for Personnel and other top management team members	. May-June 1972
. Personnel Office . Top management team . Directors and department heads	. June-July 1972
. Assistant University Librarian for Personnel	. April 1972
. Assistant University Librarian for Personnel . Other staff as appropriate	. May-July 1972
. Assistant University Librarian for Personnel	. July 1972-June 1973
. Vice President and University Librarian and the Assistant University Librarian for Planning	. March-April 1972
. Assistant University Librarian for Personnel	. September 1972-June 1973

EXHIBIT 43 (7)

Recommendation	Action To Be Taken
. Utilize multiple reporting relationships wherever appropriate to best draw upon specialized staff skills where and when they are needed	. List individuals to be assigned for part of their time in different units, and negotiate division of responsibilities and time among the respective members of the top management team
	. Prepare guidelines for working and reporting relationships among staff with shared time between different organization units, and orient individual staff accordingly
. Establish performance goals among library components and use for monitoring progress and setting goals	. Draft and review initial statement of performance criteria as part of group and unit descriptions
	. Develop specific techniques and approaches to measure performance in each major group and unit
	. Sample survey to test adequacy of performance measures for selected units and establish schedule for regular monitoring of progress
. Establish and install a comprehensive and systematic planning process throughout the libraries	. Develop planning schedule for submission and review of long- and short-term plans, specifying unit responsibility for planning product
	. Develop standard planning format in which plans should be submitted
	. Work with key staff to explain the planning process so it can be well understood and can produce desired product
. Work toward a program budget approach and format	. Consistent with university budget requirements, develop program budget format that top management group can begin to use in interpreting financial resource requirements of the adopted short-term plans
	. Hold staff meetings to identify cost factors to be included in each program area
	. Establish budget schedule and sequence for submission and review of annual budget requests under the proposed plan of organization

By Whom	Completion Date
. Assistant University Librarian for Personnel . Members of top management team	. June-July 1972
. Personnel Office . Associate and Assistant University Librarians, Directors, and department heads, as appropriate	. June-July 1972
. Vice President and University Librarian and the Associate and Assistant University Librarians . Directors and department heads . Implementation groups	. May-July 1972
. Planning Office and top management group	. July-October 1972
. Planning Office	. November 1972-January 1973
. Assistant University Librarian for Planning . Top management team	. August-September 1972
. Planning Office	. September 1972
. Planning Office	. September-October 1972
. Assistant University Librarian for Planning . University budget officials . Associate and Assistant University Librarians	. October-November 1972
. Vice President and University Librarian and the top management team . Directors and department heads	. November-December 1972
. Assistant University Librarian for Planning	. March-April 1972

EXHIBIT 43 (8)

Recommendation	Action To Be Taken
. Strengthen approaches to leadership and supervision	. Develop position statements identifying principles of leadership that should be observed by managerial and supervisory staff to maximize their units' capabilities
	. Hold staff meetings to present concepts of supervision and leadership with emphasis on staff development techniques
	. Distribute reading list of materials for managerial and supervisory staff use
. Strengthen lines of communication and use of staff input in decision making	. Establish intent to utilize staff groups and committees where appropriate to react to problems and solutions in order to gain the benefit of their thoughts prior to reaching decisions
. Install sound plans for fostering staff development and growth	. Prepare staff development plans defining approaches to career progression, guidelines for individual plans, etc.
	. Prepare and initiate schedule and roster for staff review and appraisal system to guide efforts of the Professional Advisory Committee and managerial and supervisory staff
	. Begin preparation of individual staff development plans in accordance with the schedule of staff reviews and appraisals

By Whom	Completion Date
. Assistant University Librarian for Personnel	. June 1972
. Assistant University Librarian for Personnel . Other Associate and Assistant University Librarians . Directors and department heads	. August-October 1972
. Personnel Office	. July-August 1972
. Vice President and University Librarian and the top management team	. September 1972 on
. Personnel Office	. August-September 1972
. Personnel Office	. October 1972 on
. Personnel Office	. October 1972 on

At an early date, the Vice President and University Librarian and his cabinet should establish appropriate committees and advisory groups to help them in implementation. First, the Professional Advisory Committee and the Personnel Development Committee should be established, as recommended in Chapter II. The Professional Advisory Committee and its subcommittees should be a primary means to involve staff members in implementation planning. While these committees may present their own alternatives and suggestions, they should be used principally to review and refine materials developed by the Vice President and University Librarian and his key staff members. Initial formulation of materials by staff will be better than leaving the task to committees, and the time of the committees will be used more effectively.

The Professional Advisory and Personnel Development Committees should be active throughout implementation planning in the formulation of policies, overall unit descriptions, and personnel plans. These committees can also help resolve difficulties that arise as implementation takes place. Other implementation groups set up on an *ad hoc* basis may also be useful where specialized concerns emerge. The Associate and Assistant University Librarians, in consultation with the Vice President and University Librarian, should freely draw upon such groups for help in their work.

The Representative Committee of Librarians has been successful in providing staff members with an effective forum for airing their views. This positive role should be continued during implementation in order to reflect staff concerns that may arise.

MANAGEMENT TRAINING OF STAFF

Early in the process of implementation, the Vice President and University Librarian and his top management team should identify the staff training needed to implement and work with the proposed plans effectively. Mention has already been made of multiple reporting relationships, supervisory techniques, and other matters such as meaningful staff participation where efforts should be made to improve staff understanding and performance. The personnel officer should develop and coordinate training for staff in these and other areas.

A valuable first step would be to hold several general seminars for executive and supervisory staff concerning a range of management topics. These seminars would examine broad principles of management and their particular application to research libraries. The seminars should stress the concept of management by objectives—i.e., striving to achieve specific performance goals that have been set—broadly for the overall library system and its major units and narrowly for individual staff members.

Executive and supervisory staff should at least be exposed to more expansive and dynamic views of their roles (vis-à-vis their subordinates) than they generally hold at present. They should be cognizant of the importance of their role in helping subordinates to develop individually and in constantly seeking ways to improve the libraries' services to users. While executive and supervisory staff must be certain that subordinates carry their weight and abide by established policies, they must give more attention to motivating staff and improving productivity than to enforcing rules. The libraries should sponsor training programs for staff members to learn about group dynamics and other aspects of mobilizing staff resources effectively. Seminars and other training programs should'be preceded by suggested readings in specific management areas.

Columbia's libraries do not have the resources to develop their own sophisticated training capabilities. Rather, they should draw upon the faculties of the university to assist in designing and carrying out programs. The Personnel Office should develop, as feasible, a series of basic educational programs for incoming staff members and for individuals assuming new positions of responsibility. Although some continuing training efforts may eventually be staffed by the Personnel Office, the library system should seek assistance from trained professionals within the university whose academic careers are concerned with various aspects of management and who can also offer the insight of an objective third party.

STAFF GOALS AND ASSIGNMENTS

Considerably more information on staff training and career interests
will need to be obtained for implementation than is presently available. To capitalize on individual motivations and talents, the Personnel Office should survey staff members to identify those who are
qualified and desire to work in the services, resources, or other
areas. This information should be collected as quickly as possible
and analyzed to ascertain what staffing assignments might be made
in the proposed plans. Survey results should be made available
to top management for consideration in their planning.

Several years will probably be required for personnel assignments
to conform to the proposed staffing plan. The competencies needed
to deal adequately with all the major subject areas for collection
development, in-depth reference, and research assistance are not
likely to be available at present. These gaps should be reflected
in the survey results to that recruitment plans can be made to develop
the needed staff capabilities quickly.

Another problem is the need for gradual realignment of librarian
and specialist positions. The number of librarians will be reduced
as the plan is implemented and specialist positions are filled.
However, this adjustment should consider both professional staff
presently in the library system and specialists to be trained for
specific library positions.

POLICIES, UNIT DESCRIPTIONS, AND
WORKING RELATIONSHIPS

One of the first tasks undertaken by the Vice President and University
Librarian and his top management team should be the formulation
of clear policies and concise unit descriptions to govern and guide
the new structure. These statements should constitute the beginnings
of a comprehensive policy manual that should be reviewed and
updated regularly during implementation and thereafter. Draft statements developed by the top management team should be submitted
to the Professional Advisory Committee, the Representative Committee of Librarians, and other appropriate groups for review and

comment. Such staff involvement will considerably heighten awareness and understanding of the proposed changes as well as facilitate
the implementation process.

Specifically, policy statements should be formulated in such areas
as:

- User privileges concerning the use of (1) collections and (2)
  instructional and in-depth research and reference assistance
- Collection development methods and tools
- Personnel recruitment, orientation, and career development
- Planning and budgeting
- Continuing education
- Staff grievances and appeals
- Working relationships with university officials, faculty, and
  student groups

Executives of each major group and organizational unit should
prepare unit descriptions in a standard format to cover such areas
as:

- Unit title and group
- Executive staff responsibility
- Principal role and objectives
- Key functions and responsibilities
- Reporting relationships
- Key working relationships
- Performance criteria

POSITION DESCRIPTIONS AND
WORK REQUIREMENTS

The Personnel Office, in consultation with unit executives, should
prepare preliminary position descriptions for key positions before
the proposed plan is in operation. These descriptions will be most
important to staff assuming new responsibilities. Since the descriptions will be formulated before actual work experience is gained,
they will need to be refined after the plan becomes operational.

PERFORMANCE CRITERIA

The top management team should also establish early the broad performance criteria for each group and unit mentioned in the section on policies above. These criteria will help staff to focus efforts effectively and to understand the accomplishments expected of the new structures for organization and staffing.

This chapter concludes the final report on organization and staffing of the Columbia libraries. The Vice President and University Librarian and his key staff should carefully review the approach for implementing the study recommendations which has been presented in this chapter, and modify and supplement it to make it theirs.

Appendix A

IMPLICATIONS OF SELECTED TRENDS IN HIGHER EDUCATION FOR THE ORGANIZATION AND STAFFING OF UNIVERSITY LIBRARIES

SELECTED TRENDS IN HIGHER EDUCATION	IMPLICATIONS FOR ORGANIZATION AND STAFFING OF LIBRARIES
SOCIETY'S REQUIREMENTS AND EXPECTATIONS ARE CHANGING MORE RAPIDLY THAN DURING ANY OTHER PERIOD IN HISTORY	UNIVERSITIES AND THEIR LIBRARIES WILL HAVE TO BE ORGANIZED SO THAT (1) PLANS FOR UNIVERSITY DEVELOPMENT INCLUDE PLANS FOR LIBRARIES AND (2) KEY LIBRARY STAFF PARTICIPATE IN UNIVERSITY PLANNING
The Role of the University in Society Is Changing and the University Is Under Increasing Pressure To Change Its Role	*Libraries Will Need To Be Organized To Participate in and Contribute to Planning for the University's Changing Role*

Universities are expected to:

- *Increase their relevance to society* by contributing to its advancement on a comprehensive basis, giving particular emphasis to the solution of contemporary problems, and at the same time . . .
- *Maintain their integrity* by serving society broadly while remaining independent of undue influence from any one segment.

187

Society Expects the University To Maintain a Balance Among Instruction, Research, and Community Service Activities by:

- *Providing instruction* to greater numbers of students due to increasing population and the higher proportion of the population that seeks advanced education. Equality of access and even free access to higher education are demanded. A growing proportion of the population will require continuing education to avoid cultural and professional obsolescence during their lifetimes.
- *Sponsoring research* that will contribute to human knowledge and aid in solving contemporary problems. These problems, which are increasingly concerned with urban life and preservation of the environment, are complex, requiring interdisciplinary approaches and major team efforts.
- *Providing community service* to meet the needs and expectations of the community in which the university is located rather than those services incidental to instruction and research. Urban universities are increasingly called upon to serve their urban areas.

Libraries Will Have To Be Organized and Staffed To Participate in University Planning of Instruction, Research, and Community Service Programs

Expectations Concerning Broad Constituent Participation in University Decision Making Are Increasing

Universities are called upon to:

- *Involve members of the academic community* (faculty, students, professional staff members, and others) in planning and decision making. There is increasing insistence that governing boards and the university administration not have exclusive authority for decisions and that their proceedings be open.
- *Involve individuals from outside the academic community* in planning and decision making. Requests and demands for participation are being presented by alumni, individuals and groups that reside in the area adjacent to and / or served by the institution, professional and employee organizations, members of the executive and legislative branches of government, and others.

Provision Will Need To Be Made To Involve Library Staff Members in Library Planning and Decision Making and in University-Wide Planning and Decision Making

SELECTED TRENDS IN HIGHER EDUCATION	IMPLICATIONS FOR ORGANIZATION AND STAFFING OF LIBRARIES

Group Strength Is Being Used Forcefully To Present Requirements, Expectations, and Demands to Universities

Libraries Will Need To Be Organized and Staffed To Communicate and Negotiate Effectively With a Wide Variety of Groups

Universities are being called upon to work effectively with groups of:

- *Students* organized on the basis of academic levels, academic fields, extrauniversity interests, racial origin, etc.
- *Faculty* organized on similar bases, in some instances in concert with students.
- *Employees* organized in unions and/or on bases similar to those of students and faculty.
- *Community representatives* organized to get the university to serve their needs or meet their demands in a variety of fields.
- *Others* who see the university as a source of benefit or as an opponent to their aspirations.

Both Public and Private Universities Are Increasingly Expected To Become Financially Responsible and Effective by:

Libraries, Like Other University Components, Will Have To Be Organized and Staffed To Plan and Control Budgets and Costs

- *Increasing cost effectiveness.*
- *Expanding services* with available resources.

UNIVERSITY PHILOSOPHIES AND OBJECTIVES ARE BEING REVISED TO RELATE UNIVERSITIES MORE CLOSELY AND EFFECTIVELY TO SOCIETY AS A WHOLE

UNIVERSITIES AND THEIR LIBRARIES WILL NEED TO BE ORGANIZED AND STAFFED TO ALLOW CHANGES TO BE MADE IN EMPHASIS IN THEIR PHILOSOPHIES AND OBJECTIVES

Universities Consider That They Are Responsible for Providing Leadership and Aid in Meeting Society's Requirements and Expectations

Libraries Will Need To Be Organized and Staffed To (1) Recognize Pressing and Valid Needs That Call for Library Attention and/or Participation, (2) Plan Creative and Effective Programs and Services, and (3) Carry Out These Programs and Services

Limited Financial Resources Are Forcing Universities To Establish Limited Objectives

Libraries Will Need To Be Organized and Staffed To Enable Effective Programs and Services To Be (1) Planned With Care, Prudence, and Attention to Priorities and (2) Carried Out With Limited Financial Resources

- *Quantitative limits are being set* to allow educational quality to be maintained, wherever possible.
- *Priorities are being established* among objectives to allow quality to be maintained in most important areas.

UNIVERSITY PROGRAMS ARE BEING CHANGED IN EMPHASIS AND APPROACH

LIBRARIES WILL NEED TO BE ORGANIZED AND STAFFED TO (1) SUPPORT PROGRAMS DIFFERENT FROM THOSE IN THE PAST AND (2) DEVELOP AND USE NEW APPROACHES

SELECTED TRENDS IN HIGHER EDUCATION	IMPLICATIONS FOR ORGANIZATION AND STAFFING OF LIBRARIES
Universities Are Shifting the Relative Emphasis Given to Programs	*Libraries Will Need To Be Organized Flexibly To (1) Perceive Program Changes and the Contribution Libraries Can Make and (2) Accommodate to Changes in Program Emphasis*
Programs of Instruction Are Being Revised	The libraries will need to be organized and staffed to support changing programs of instruction. Specialized staff will need to be provided to: • Orient and assist students who will be expected to make greater use of library resources at undergraduate and graduate levels. • Assist those interested in continuing education by maintaining bibliographies and introducing them to new library resources. • Develop, maintain, and facilitate the use of library resources peculiar to the urban affairs field and the university locale.
Research Programs Are Being Revised at Most Universities	The libraries will need to be organized and have specialized staff to: • Assist those engaged in research in new and rapidly changing fields. • Assist multidisciplinary teams to draw upon library resources in many fields. • Aid in gaining access to library resources on a minimum cost basis. • Provide in-depth sophisticated subject reference assistance to those engaged in research.
Community Service Programs Are Becoming More Important	The libraries will need to be organized and have the specialized staff to support urban community service programs by providing: • Access to the multidisciplinary resources needed. • Assistance to individuals at numerous locations who have limited skill and experience in making use of library resources.
UNIVERSITIES ARE UNDERGOING RAPID AND CONTINUING CHANGES IN THE WAYS IN WHICH THEY ARE ORGANIZED AND STAFFED *Most Universities Have Revised Their Plans of Organization in Recent Years and Anticipate Further Revisions*	LIBRARIES WILL NEED TO BE (1) RELATED ORGANIZATIONALLY TO THE REST OF THE UNIVERSITY AT THE HIGHEST LEVELS, (2) INTIMATELY RELATED TO THE FACULTY, AND (3) ORGANIZED INTERNALLY TO WORK EFFECTIVELY WITH OTHER COMPONENTS OF THE UNIVERSITY

SELECTED TRENDS IN HIGHER EDUCATION	IMPLICATIONS FOR ORGANIZATION AND STAFFING OF LIBRARIES

- *Redistributing responsibilities* among the governing board, faculty, students, and administration has been general. New and modified approaches—such as the establishment of more comprehensive university senates—have been adopted.
- *Restructuring top management* has been common. The size, composition, and committee structures of governing boards are being changed. Top administration structures are being established, presidential cabinets are being used more effectively, and senior executives with broader experience are being appointed.

The university libraries should be linked effectively at the highest level to the other components of the university having responsibilities for programs of instruction, research, and community service.

University libraries should be organized internally to accommodate easily to changes in the way in which other components of the university are organized.

University Staffing Is Changing Significantly

Patterns of Library Staffing Should Be Changed To (1) Correspond to University Changes and (2) Meet Distinctive Library Requirements

Most Universities, Including Columbia, Are Seeking Ways To Increase Faculty Productivity

- Increasing use is being made of instructors and teaching assistants.
- Efforts are being made to increase teaching loads and class size.
- Some offerings are being eliminated at some institutions to increase class size and reduce faculty work load.

The libraries should be organized and staffed to help increase faculty productivity by (1) providing faculty members with needed services and assistance and (2) augmenting the efforts by instructing and assisting students to make use of library resources.

New Specialized Professional and Technical Staff Positions Are Being Established

- *Medical institutions* are adding semi-professional and technical positions.
- *Research units* are making greater use of technicians with specialized skills.
- *Libraries* are adding bibliographers and other specialized professionals as well as workers with technical and administrative skills
- *Computer centers* and units making use of computers are adding skilled professional and technical workers.

Libraries should seek to develop new skilled positions to (1) meet new and emerging needs and (2) maximize the productivity of faculty members and senior members of the library staff.

Turnover of Staff Continues High in Nearly All Fields and at All Levels

- Competent *executives* are difficult to recruit. They continue in positions for very short periods of time.

Libraries will need to (1) develop and maintain continuing contacts in fields that will be useful for recruitment of replacement staff and (2) orient and give in-service training to staff at all levels on a continuing basis.

SELECTED TRENDS IN HIGHER EDUCATION	IMPLICATIONS FOR ORGANIZATION AND STAFFING OF LIBRARIES
• *Faculty* mobility continues high, with loyalty frequently given to an academic field rather than to an institution. • *Professional workers*, such as librarians, are mobile. • *Technical and unskilled workers* in all fields change jobs frequently in pursuit of greater opportunities and compensation.	Libraries will need to give greater emphasis to personnel and professional development both to enhance staff capabilities and to provide meaningful opportunities for growth and achievement.
UNIVERSITIES ARE FACED WITH INCREASING FACILITIES CONSTRAINTS AT THE SAME TIME THAT THEIR REQUIREMENTS ARE INCREASING AND CHANGING	UNIVERSITIES WILL HAVE TO BE ORGANIZED AND STAFFED TO DEVELOP AND MAINTAIN THEIR COLLECTIONS AND PROGRAMS WITHIN LIMITED FACILITIES AT A TIME WHEN (1) SPACE REQUIREMENTS ARE INCREASING RAPIDLY AND (2) TECHNOLOGICAL ADVANCES MAKE NEW AND DIFFERENT FACILITIES ESSENTIAL
AMERICAN UNIVERSITIES ARE FACED WITH GROWING FINANCIAL CRISES	RAPIDLY INCREASING LIBRARY COSTS REQUIRE THAT LIBRARIES (1) BE ORGANIZED FOR MAXIMUM COST EFFECTIVENESS, (2) HAVE PATTERNS OF STAFFING THAT ALLOW THE HIGHEST SKILLS OF STAFF MEMBERS TO BE USED FULLY, AND (3) HAVE LEADERSHIP AND SUPERVISION THAT HELP ENSURE HIGH PRODUCTIVITY
Universities Generally Are Faced With: • *Increasing costs* of operation and for capital development. • *Restricted growth in income* from public and private sources. • *Tuition and fee limitations* that preclude meeting growing deficits by increasing tuition rates.	Libraries will need to be organized and staffed to (1) work closely with the university's top administration in budget planning, (2) develop sound library budgets related to university program plans, (3) control budgets and costs carefully, and (4) expand financing sources wherever possible.
University Library Costs Are Increasing Across the Nation • *Costs of maintaining and developing collections* are increasing due to: —*The great volume* of books, serials, and other materials produced each year. —*Purchasing practices* that call for automatic purchase of materials. —*Increasing prices* for new items as well as for scarce, out-of-print, and original items.	Libraries will need to be organized and staffed to (1) achieve increasing and maximum productivity in the use of both personal services and mechanized, electronic, and other technological aids and (2) participate effectively in university efforts to develop and utilize additional sources of financing, including both private and government sources.

- *Processing costs* are increasing due to the high proportion of labor costs to total costs and to rising compensation rates.
- *Operating costs* generally are increasing due to the high proportion of labor costs to total costs and to rising compensation rates.
- *Columbia's library costs* are increasing at a more rapid rate than those of most university libraries due to local cost levels and union pressures.

THERE IS GROWING RECOGNITION OF THE NEED FOR CLOSER WORKING RELATIONSHIPS AMONG UNIVERSITIES AND OTHER INSTITUTIONS TO AVOID UNDESIRABLE DUPLICATION AND TO SHARE AVAILABLE SCARCE RESOURCES

Major Universities Are Seeking Ways To Cooperate More Effectively To Avoid Unnecessary Duplication of Specialized Academic Programs and Library Collections

LIBRARIES WILL NEED TO BE ORGANIZED AND STAFFED TO PLAN AND IMPLEMENT SCHEMES OF INTERINSTITUTIONAL AND REGIONAL COOPERATION

Libraries will need to be organized and staffed to (1) maintain and improve working relations with other libraries, (2) devise and expand other means of collective use of materials and facilities, and (3) support and encourage development of interinstitutional and other cooperative means of extending access to distinctive collections.

Appendix B

**SELECTED BIBLIOGRAPHY FOR THE STUDY OF
ORGANIZATION AND STAFFING OF
COLUMBIA LIBRARIES**

General Materials—Corporate

Ackoff, Russel L. *A Concept of Corporate Planning*. New York: Wiley-Interscience, 1970.

Argyris, Chris. *Management and Organizational Development*. New York: McGraw-Hill, 1971.

Churchman, Charles West. *The Systems Approach*. New York: Delacorte Press, 1968.

Dale, Ernest. *Management: Theory and Practice*. 2nd ed. New York: McGraw-Hill, 1969.

Drucker, Peter F. *Managing for Results*. New York: Harper and Row, 1964.

Drucker, Peter F. "What We Can Learn From Japanese Management." *Harvard Business Review,* March-April, 1971, pp. 110+.

Goetz, Billy Earl. *Quantitative Methods: A Survey and Guide for Managers*. New York: McGraw-Hill, 1965.

Koontz, Harold. "Making Sense of Management Theory." *Harvard Business Review,* July-August, 1962, p. 25.

Koontz, Harold D. and O'Donnell, Cyril J. *Principles of Management: An Analysis of Managerial Functions*. 4th ed. New York: McGraw-Hill, 1968.

Koontz, Harold, ed. *Toward a Unified Theory of Management*. New York: McGraw-Hill, 1964.

Lazzaro, Victor, ed. *Systems and Procedures: A Handbook for Business and Industry*. 2nd ed. Englewood Cliffs, New Jersey: Prentice Hall, 1968.

Likert, Rensis. *New Patterns of Management*. New York: McGraw-Hill, 1961.

Likert, Rensis. *The Human Organization: Its Management and Value*. New York: McGraw-Hill, 1967.

McGregor, Douglas. *The Human Side of Enterprise*. New York: McGraw-Hill, 1960.

Mann, Roland, ed. *The Arts of Top Management: A McKinsey Anthology*. New York: McGraw-Hill, 1971.

Marrow, A. J., Bowers, D.G., and Seashore, S.E. "Management by Participation: Creating a Climate for Personal and Organizational Development." *Contemporary Psychology,* March, 1969, pp. 74–75.

Maurer, Herrymon. "Management by Committee." *Fortune,* April, 1953, pp. 145+.

194

Maynard, Harold B., ed. *Handbook of Business Administration*. New York: McGraw-Hill, 1967.

Miller, Ernest C. *Management by Objectives and the Use of Performance Standards*. Jersey City: American Management Association, 1965.

Millet, John D. *Management in the Public Service: The Quest for Effective Performance*. New York: McGraw-Hill, 1954.

Newman, William H. and Summer, Charles E. Jr., *The Process of Management: Concepts, Behavior and Practice*. Englewood Cliffs, New Jersey: Prentice-Hall, 1961.

Pigors, Paul, Malm, F. T., and Myers, Charles A., eds. *Management of Human Resources*. 2nd. ed. New York: McGraw-Hill, 1969.

Rush, Harold M. F. *Behavioral Science: Concepts and Management Application*. Studies in Personnel Policy No. 216. New York: National Industrial Conference Board, 1969.

Sampson, Robert C. *Managing the Managers: A Realistic Approach to Applying the Behavioral Sciences*. New York: McGraw-Hill, 1965.

Schick, Allen. *Budget Innovation in the States*. Washington, D.C.: The Brookings Institution, 1971.

Scott, William G. *Human Relations in Management: A Behavioral Science Approach: Philosophy Analysis and Issues*. Homewood, Illinois: Richard Irwin, 1962.

Simon, Herman A. "The Proverbs of Administration." *Public Administration Review*, Winter, 1964, pp. 53–57.

Starr, Martin K. *Management: A Modern Approach*. New York: Harcourt, Brace, Jovanovich, 1971.

Steiner, George A. *Top Management Planning*. London, England: The MacMillan Company, 1969.

Whitehead, Clay Thomas. *Uses and Limitations of Systems Analysis*. Santa Monica, California: The Rand Corporation. 1967.

Weisbard, M. R. "Management in Crisis." (An Interview with Dr. Likert) *The Conference Board Record*, February, 1970, pp. 10–16.

General Material—Higher Education

Barzun, Jacques. *The American University: How It Runs and Where It Is Going*. New York: Harper and Row, 1968.

Bell, Daniel. *The Reforming of Formal Education: The Columbia Experience in Its National Setting*. New York: Columbia University Press, 1966.

Brameld, Theodore B. H. *Education for the Emerging Age: Newer Ends and Stronger Means*. New York: Harper and Row, 1965.

Brien, R. H. "The Managerialization of Higher Education." *Educational Record*, Summer, 1970, pp. 273–280.

Brown, James Douglas. *The Liberal University: An Institutional Analysis*. New York: McGraw-Hill, 1969.

Brubacher, John S. and Rudy, Willis. *Higher Education in Transition, A History of American Colleges and Universities*, 2d ed. New York: Harper and Row, 1968.

Jencks, Christoper and Riesman, David. *The Academic Revolution*. New York: Doubleday, 1968.

Millet, John D. *The Academic Community: An Essay on Organization*. New York: McGraw-Hill, 1962.

Russell, John D. "Changing Patterns of Administrative Organization in Higher Education." *The Annals of the American Academy of Political and Social Sciences*, September, 1955, pp. 26–27.

Silberman, Charles E. *Crisis in the Classroom: The Remaking of American Education*. New York: Random House, 1970.

Simon, K. A. and Fullam, M. G. *Projections of Educational Statistics to 1977-78*. Washington, D. C.: Government Printing Office, 1969.

196   **Appendix B**

General Materials—Libraries

Asheim, Lester, ed. *Persistent Issues in American Librarianship.* Chicago: University of Chicago, Graduate Library School, 1961.

American Council of Learned Societies. *Use, Misuse, and Nonuse of Academic Libraries.* College and University Library Section, New York Library Association, 1970.

American Library Association. *Library Statistics: A Handbook of Concepts, Definitions and Terminology.* Chicago, Illinois: American Library Association, 1966.

Association of College and Research Libraries. "A.L.A. Standards for College Libraries." *College and Research Libraries,* July, 1959, pp. 274–280.

Association of Research Libraries. "Academic Library Statistics: 1969/70." Washington, D.C.: Association of Research Libraries, 1970.

Bellomy, Fred L. "Management Planning for Library Systems Development." *Journal of Library Automation.* December, 1969, pp. 187–217.

Booz, Allen & Hamilton, Inc. *Problems in University Library Management.* Washington, D.C.: Association of Research Libraries, 1971.

Branscomb, Lewis C. "Libraries in Larger Institutions of Higher Education." *Library Trends.* October, 1961, pp. 179–196.

Bryant, Douglas W. "University Libraries and the Future." *Library Association Record,* January, 1966, pp. 2–8.

Buck, Paul H. *Libraries and Universities: Addresses and Reports.* Cambridge: Belknap Press of Harvard University Press, 1964.

Buck, Paul. "Problems and Objectives of a Great Research Library." *Library Journal,* June, 1961, pp. 2051–2056.

Buckland, Michael K. et. al. *Systems Analysis of a University Library: Final Report on a Research Project.* Lancaster, England: University of Lancaster, 1970.

Cameron, Donald F. and Heim, Peggy. *The Economics of Librarianship in College and University Libraries, 1969–70.* Washington, D.C.: Council on Library Resources, Inc., 1970.

Castagna, Edwin. *National Inventory of Library Needs.* Chicago: American Library Association, 1965.

Clapp, Verner W. *The Future of the Research Library.* Urbana: University of Illinois Press, 1964.

Commager, Henry S. "Crisis of the Academic Library." *Wilson Library Bulletin,* February, 1969, pp. 518–525.

Committee on Research Libraries. *On Research Libraries; Statement and Recommendations.* Cambridge: M.I.T. Press, 1969.

Dix, William S. "New Challenges to University Libraries." *University: A Princeton Quarterly.* Fall, 1965, pp. 3–16.

Dougherty, Richard M. and Heinritz, Fred J. *Scientific Management of Library Operations.* New York: Scarecrow Press, 1966.

Downs, Robert B. *University Library Statistics.* Washington, D.C.: Association of Research Libraries, 1969.

Drott, M. Carl. "Random Sampling: A Tool for Library Research." *College and Research Libraries,* March, 1969, pp. 119–125.

Dunn, Oliver C., Siebert, W.F., and Scheuneman, Janice. *The Past and Likely Future of 58 Research Libraries: 1951—1980: A Statistical Study of Growth and Change.* Lafayette, Indiana: Purdue University, 1969.

Ellsworth, Ralph E. "Trends in Higher Education Affecting the College and University Library." *Library Trends,* 1951, pp. 8–19.

Fussler, Herman H. and Simon, Julian L. *Patterns in the Use of Books in Large Research Libraries.* Chicago: University of Chicago Press, 1969.

Fussler, Herman H., ed. *The Function of the Library in the Modern College.* The Nineteenth Annual Conference of the Graduate Library School, June 14–18, 1954. Chicago, Illinois: University of Chicago Press, 1967.

Heinritz, Fred J. "Quantitative Management in Libraries." *College and Research Libraries,* July, 1970, pp. 232–238.

Josey, Elonnie J. "Community Use of Academic Libraries." *Library Trends,* July, 1969, pp. 66–74.

Kellam, William P. and Barker, D. L. "Activities and Opportunities of University Librarians for Full Participation in the Educational Enterprise." *College and Research Libraries,* May, 1968, pp. 195–199.

Kemper, Robert E. *Library Management, Behavior-Based Personnel Systems (BBPS): A Framework for Analysis,* Littleton, Colorado: Libraries Unlimited, 1971.

Knight, Douglas M., and Nourse, E. Shepley, eds. *Libraries at Large: Tradition, Innovation and the National Interest.* New York: Bowker, 1969.

Leimkuhler, Ferdinand F. "Systems Analysis in Libraries." *College and Research Libraries,* January, 1966, pp. 13–18.

Licklider, Joseph C.R. *Libraries of the Future.* Cambridge: M.I.T. Press, 1965.

Line, Maurice B. "University Libraries and the Information Needs of the Researcher: A Provider's View." *Aslib Proceedings,* July, 1966, pp. 178–184.

Lowell, Mildred H. *The Management of Libraries and Information Centers, Volumes I and II.* Metuchen, New Jersey: The Scarecrow Press, 1968.

Lyle, Guy R. *The Administration of the College Library,* 3d ed. New York: Wilson, 1961.

Mackenzie, A. Graham and Stuart, Ian M., eds. *Planning Library Services: Proceedings of a Research Seminar Held at the University of Lancaster, July 9–11, 1969.* Lancaster, England: University of Lancaster Libraries, 1969.

Mason, Ellsworth G. "Along the Academic Way: A Report of a Seven-Month Study Project, November 1, 1969 to May 31, 1970." Funded by a Council on Library Resources Fellowship. *Library Journal,* May, 1971, pp. 1671–1676.

Meier, R. L. "Efficiency Criteria for the Operation of Large Libraries." *Library Quarterly,* July, 1961, pp. 215–234.

Morelock, Molete and Leimkuhler, Ferdinand F. "Library Operations Research and Systems Engineering Studies." *College and Research Libraries,* November, 1964, pp. 501–503.

Mohrhardt, Foster E. "Office of the Librarian." *Wilson Library Bulletin,* December, 1967, pp. 391–396.

Moon, Eric and Nyren, Karl, eds. *Library Issues: The Sixties.* New York: R.R. Bowker Co., 1970.

Morse, Philip. "Probabilistic Models for Library Operations." In Association of Research Libraries, *Minutes of the Sixty-Third Meeting, January 26, 1964.* Washington, D.C.: Association of Research Libraries, 1964.

Mumford, Lewis Quincy. "Library Administration in its Current Development." *Library Trends,* 1959, p. 358.

Munn, Robert F. "Bottomless Pit or the Academic Library as Viewed From the Administration Building." *College and Research Libraries,* January, 1968, pp. 51–54.

Pings, Vern M. "The Library as a Social Agency, Response to Social Change." *College and Research Libraries,* May, 1970, pp. 174–184.

Radford, Neil A. "Problems of Academic Library Statistics." *Library Quarterly,* July, 1968, pp. 231–248.

Reece, Ernest J. "Current Trends in Library Administration." *Library Trends,* January, 1959, pp. 331–491.

Robinson, Eric E. "Developments in Higher Education and Their Implications for Libraries." *Library Association Record,* May, 1969, pp. 142–143.

Rogers, Rutherford D. and Weber, David C. *University Library Administration.* New York: H.W. Wilson, 1971.

Shaw, Ralph R. "Scientific Management in the Library." *Library Association Bulletin,* Fall, 1956, pp. 97–101.

Stone, Elizabeth W. *Training for the Improvement of Library Administration.* Urbana: University of Illinois, Graduate School of Library Science, 1967.

Tauber, Maurice F. *Technical Services in Libraries*. New York: Columbia University Press, 1954.

Voigt, Melvin L., ed. *Advances in Librarianship, Volume I*. New York: Academic Press, 1970.

Vosper, Robert G. "Libraries and the Inquiring Mind." *ALA Bulletin*, September, 1965, pp. 709–717.

Wasserman, Paul. "Development of Administration in Library Service: Current Status and Future Prospects." *College and Research Libraries*, 1958, pp. 284–285.

Wasserman, Paul. *The Librarian and the Machine*. Detroit: Gale Research Company, 1965.

Wessel, C.J. and Cohrssen, B.A. *Criteria for Evaluating the Effectiveness of Library Operation and Services: Phase I: Literature Search and State of the Art*. Washington, D.C.: John I. Thompson and Co., 1967.

Wilson, Louis Round and Rauber, Maurice F. *The University Library: The Organization, Administration, and Functions of Academic Libraries*. 2nd ed. New York: Columbia University Press, 1956.

Organization—Corporate

Argyris, Chris. "The Organization: What Makes it Healthy?" *Harvard Business Review*, November-December, 1958, pp. 107–116.

Argyris, Chris. "Organizational Effectiveness Under Stress." *Harvard Business Review*, May-June, 1960, pp. 137–145.

Argyris, Chris. *Organization and Innovation*. Homewood, Illinois: Richard D. Irwin, 1965.

Barkdull, C. W. "Span of Control—A Method of Evaluation." *Michigan Business Review*, May, 1963, pp. 25–32.

Bassett, G.A. and Hawk, R.H. "Function and Dysfunction in the Organization." *Personnel*, September-October, 1965, pp. 23–31.

Bennis, Warren G. *Changing Organizations*. New York: McGraw-Hill, 1966.

Blake, Robert R. "Breakthrough in Organization Development." *Harvard Business Review*, November-December, 1964, pp. 133–135.

Chapple, Eliot D. and Sayles, Leonard R. *The Measure of Management: Designing Organization for Human Effectiveness*. New York: MacMillan, 1961.

Cooper, William W., Leavitt, H.J. and Shelly, M.W. *New Perspectives in Organization Research*. New York: John Wiley and Sons, 1964.

Cummings, L.L. and Scott, W.E. *Readings in Organizational Behavior and Human Performance*. Homewood, Illinois: Richard D. Irwin, Inc., 1969.

Dale, Ernest. *The Great Organizers*. New York: McGraw-Hill, 1960.

Dale, Ernest. *Planning and Developing the Company Organization Structure*. New York: American Management Association, 1952.

Dale, Ernest, and Urwick, L. *Staff in Organization*. New York: McGraw-Hill, 1960.

Flory, C.D. "The Imperatives of Authority." *Dun's Review and Modern Industry*. February, 1965. pp. 49–50+.

Golembiewski, Robert T. "Organization as a Moral Problem." *Public Administration Review*, Spring, 1962, pp. 51–58.

Hampton, David R., Summer, Charles E. and Webber, Ross A. *Organizational Behavior and the Practice of Management*. Glenview, Illinois: Scott, Foresman, 1968.

Kast, Fremont E. and Rosenzweig, James E. *Organization and Management: A Systems Approach*. New York: McGraw-Hill, 1970.

Learned, Edmund P. and Sproat, Audrey T. *Organization Theory and Policy: Notes for Analysis*. Homewood, Illinois: Richard D. Irwin, 1966.

Litterer, Joseph A. *The Analysis of Organizations*. New York: John Wiley and Sons, 1965.

Logan, Hall H. "Line and Staff: An Obsolete Concept?" *Personnel*, January-February, 1966, pp. 26–33.

March, James G., ed. *Handbook of Organizations*. Chicago: Rand McNally, 1965.

Steiner, Gary A., ed. *The Creative Organization.* Chicago, University of Chicago Press, 1965.

Tannenbaum, Arnold S., ed. *Control in Organizations.* New York: McGraw-Hill, 1968.

Thompson, James D. *Organizations in Action: Social Science Bases of Administrative Theory.* New York: McGraw-Hill, 1967.

Valentine, Raymond F. "The Rampant Organization." *Systems and Procedures Journal,* September-October, 1965, pp. 28–33.

White, Karol M. *Understanding the Company Organization Chart.* New York: American Management Association, 1963.

Organization—Libraries

Auld, Lawrence W. S. "Functional Organization Plan for Technical Services." *Library Resources and Technical Services,* Summer, 1970, pp. 458–462.

Baker, Norman R. and Nance, R. E. "Organizational Analyses and Simulation Studies of University Libraries: A Methodological Overview." *Information Storage and Retrieval.* February, 1970, pp. 153–168.

Bergen, Daniel P. "University Library Organization as a Response to University Emphases." *Library Quarterly,* January, 1962, pp. 19–39.

Brock, Clifton. "Reference Service in the Divisional Plan Library: Some Tentative Questions," *College and Research Libraries,* November, 1961, pp. 449–456.

Bruno, J.M. "Decentralization in Academic Libraries." *Library Trends,* January, 1971, pp. 311–317.

Burgis, G.C. "Systems Concept of Organization and Control for Large University Libraries." *Canadian Library Journal,* January, 1971, pp. 24–29.

Cooper, Marianne. "Organizational Patterns of Academic Science Libraries." *College and Research Libraries,* September, 1968, pp. 357–363.

Haro, Robert P. "Research Unit Libraries as Special Libraries on the Campus." *Special Libraries,* October, 1968, pp. 634–637.

Howard, Edward N. "The Orbital Organization." *Library Journal.* May 1, 1970, pp. 1712–1715.

Kaser, David. "Modernizing the University Library Structure." *College and Research Libraries,* July, 1970, pp. 227–231.

Kilpela, Raymond E.O. "Administrative Structure of the University Library." *College and Research Libraries,* November, 1968, pp. 511–516.

Kilpela, Raymond E.O. "University Library Committees." *College and Research Libraries,* March, 1968, pp. 141–143.

Legg, Jean M. "The Death of the Departmental Library." *Library Resources and Technical Services,* Summer, 1965, pp. 351–355.

McAnally, Arthur M. "Departments in University Libraries." *Library Trends,* 1959, pp. 448–464.

McCarthy, Stephen A. "Administrative Organization and Management." In Tauber, M.F. and Stephens, I.R., eds. *Library Surveys.* New York: Columbia University Press, 1967, pp. 142–156.

McCarthy, Stephen A. "Advisory Committee or Administrative Board?" *The Library Quarterly,* July, 1952, pp. 223–231.

Marchant, Maurice P. *The Effects of the Decision Making Process and Related Organizational Factors on Alternative Measures of Performance in University Libraries.* Unpublished Ph.D. Thesis. Ann Arbor: University of Michigan, 1970.

Metcalf, Keyes D. *Report on the Harvard University Library: A Study of Present and Prospective Problems.* Cambridge: Harvard University Library, 1955.

Newhall, Suzanne K. "Departmental Libraries and the Problem of Autonomy." *ALA Bulletin,* July, 1966, pp. 721–722.

Schwenn, Roger E. "Center System Libraries: The University of Wisconsin." *Wisconsin Library Bulletin,* March, 1967, pp. 85–86.

Spence, Paul H. *A Comparative Study of University Library Organizational Structure.*
Ph.D. Thesis. Urbana, Illinois: University of Illinois, 1969.
Tauber, Maurice et al. "Centralization and Decentralization in Academic Libraries: Symposium." *College and Research Libraries,* September, 1961, pp. 327–344.

Staffing—Corporate

Adelberg, Morton. "The Challenge of Today's Personnel Administration." *Personnel,*
September-October, 1965, pp. 67–70.
American Management Association. *The Systems Approach to Personnel Management.*
New York: American Management Association, 1965.
Cassell, Frank H. "Manpower Planning: The Basic Policies." *Personnel,* November-December, 1965, pp. 55–61.
Finkle, R.B. and Jones, W.S. *Assessing Corporate Talent: A Key to Managerial Manpower Planning.* New York: Wiley-Interscience, 1970.
Finley, Robert E., ed. *The Personnel Man and His Job.* New York: American Management
Association, 1962.
Gellerman, Saul W. *Motivation and Productivity.* New York: American Management
Association, 1963.
Herzberg, Frederick. "One More Time: How do you Motivate Employees?" *Harvard
Business Review,* January-February, 1968, pp. 53–62.
Kellogg, Marion S. *What to do About Performance Appraisal: An AMA Handbook.* New
York: American Management Association, 1965.
Kindall, A. F. and Gatza, J. "Positive Program for Performance Appraisal." *Harvard
Business Review,* November-December, 1963.
Levinson, Harry. *The Exceptional Executive: A Psychological Conception.* Cambridge,
Massachusetts: Harvard University Press, 1968.
Lopez, Felix M. *The Making of a Manager: Guidelines to His Selection and Promotion.*
New York: American Management Association, 1970.
Pigors, Paul and Myers, Charles A. *Personnel Administration: A Point of View and a
Method.* 6th ed. New York: McGraw-Hill, 1969.
Public Employees Relations Center. *The Crisis in Public Employee Relations in the
Decade of the Seventies.* Proceedings of a seminar conducted by Harbridge House.
February 25–27, 1970. Washington, D.C.: Bureau of National Affairs, 1970.
Strauss, George and Sayles, Leonard R. *Personnel: The Human Problems of Management.*
Englewood Cliffs, New Jersey: Prentice-Hall, 1960.

Staffing—Libraries

American Library Association. "Criteria for Programs to Prepare Library Technical Assistants." *American Library Association Bulletin,* June, 1969, pp. 787–794.
American Library Association. "Subprofessional or Technical Assistant, a Statement of
Definition." *American Library Association Bulletin,* April, 1968, pp. 387–397.
American Library Association, Board on Personnel Administration. *Personnel Organization and Procedure: A Manual Suggested for Use in College and University
Libraries.* 2nd ed. Chicago: American Library Association, 1968.
Asheim, Lester E. "Education and Manpower for Librarianship: First Steps Toward a
Statement of Policy." *American Library Association Bulletin,* October, 1968, pp.
1096–1118.
Branscomb, Lewis C., ed. *The Case for Faculty Status for Academic Librarians.* Chicago:
American Library Association, 1970.
Brown, Helen M. "Personnel and Manpower Needs of the Future." *Library Trends,*
July, 1969, pp. 75–84.
Byrd, Cecil K. "Subject Specialists in a University Library." *College and Research
Libraries,* May, 1966, pp. 191–193.

Cassata, Mary B. "Teach in: The Academic Librarian's Key to Status?" *College and Research Libraries,* January, 1970, pp. 22–27.

Corbett, Edmund V. "Staffing of Large Municipal Libraries in England and the United States: A Comparative Survey." *Journal of Librarianship,* April, 1971, pp. 83–100.

Dougherty, Richard M. "Manpower Utilization in Technical Services." *Library Resources and Technical Services,* Winter, 1968, pp. 77–82.

Drenan, Henry T. and Reed, Sarah R. "Library Manpower." *American Library Association Bulletin,* September, 1967, pp. 957–965.

Fairholm, G. W. et al. *Library Manpower: A Preliminary Study of Essential Factors Contributing to Library Staffing Patterns.* Albany: New York State Division of the Budget-State University of New York, 1968.

Fairholm, Gilbert A. "Essentials of Library Manpower Budgeting." *College and Research Libraries,* September, 1970, pp. 332–340.

Ginzberg, Eli and Brown, Carol A. *Manpower for Library Services.* New York: Conservation of Human Resources Project, Columbia University Press, 1967.

Humphreys, Kenneth W. "Subject Specialist in National and University Libraries." *Libri,* 1967, pp. 29–41.

Kemper, Robert E. *Library Management: Behavior-Based Personnel Systems (BBPS): A Framework for Analysis.* Littleton, Colorado: Libraries Unlimited, 1971.

Martin, Lowell A. "Personnel in Library Surveys." In Tauber, M.F. and Stephens, I.R., eds. *Library Surveys,* New York: Columbia University Press. 1967, pp. 123–141.

McNeal, Archie L. "Changing Personnel Patterns in College and University Libraries." *Modern Library Association Quarterly,* June, 1969, pp. 159+.

Muller, Robert H. "Principles Governing the Employment of Non-Professional Personnel in University Libraries." *College and Research Libraries,* May, 1967, pp. 2041–2046.

Moon, Eric. "Myths and Realities: The Complex But Highly Visible Manpower Problem." *Library Journal,* June 15, 1967, p. 2319.

Morrison, Perry D. *The Career of the Academic Librarian: A Study of the Social Origins, Educational Attainments, Vocational Experience and Personality Characteristics of a Group of American Academic Librarians.* Chicago: American Library Association, 1969.

Plate, Kenneth H. *Management Personnel in Libraries: A Theoretical Model for Analysis.* Rockaway, New Jersey: American Faculty Press, 1970.

Rockwood, Ruth H., ed. *Personnel Utilization in Libraries:* Selected Papers. Tallahassee, Florida: School of Library Science, Florida State University, 1970.

Schiller, Anita R. *Characteristics of Professional Personnel in College and University Libraries: Final Report.* Washington, D.C.: U.S. Office of Education, 1968.

Shaffer, Kenneth R. *Library Personnel Administration and Supervision.* 2nd ed. Hamden, Connecticut: Shoe String Press, 1963.

Smith, Eldred. "Academic Status for College and University Librarians: Problems and Prospects." *College and Research Libraries,* January, 1970, pp. 7–13.

Stebbins, Kathleen B. *Personnel Administration in Libraries,* 2nd ed. Revised by Foster Mohrhardt. New York: Scarecrow Press, 1966.

Stone, Elizabeth W., ed. "Personnel Development and Continuing Education in Libraries." *Library Trends,* July, 1971, Entire Issue.

Columbia University Libraries

Colmen, J. G. and Wheeler, B. A. *Human Uses of the University.* New York: Praeger Publishers, 1970.

Columbia University. *Directory of Officers and Staff, 1969–70,* Internal Document, 1970.

Columbia University. *The Faculty Handbook of Columbia University.* New York: Columbia University Press, 1968.

Columbia University. *Financial Reports: 1959 to Date*. New York: Columbia University.
Columbia University Budget Committee. *Comments on the Report of the Budget Review Committee Submitted to the University Senate on October 2, 1970*. Unpublished memo, October 28, 1970.
Columbia University Libraries. *Annual Reports of Library Divisions to the Director: 1960–70*. Internal Documents.
Columbia University Libraries. *Annual Report of the Director to the President: 1968–69, 1969–70*. Internal Documents.
Columbia University Libraries. *Directors Newsletter: 1970/71*. Internal Documents.
Columbia University Libraries. *Handbook*. Internal Document, 1969.
Columbia University Libraries. *Library Unit Fact Sheets*. Internal Documents, n.d.
Columbia University Libraries. *Minutes of Standing and Ad Hoc Committee, 1970/71*. Internal Documents.
Columbia University Libraries. *Staff Roster: 1970/71*. Internal Document.
Columbia University Libraries Cost Analysis Committee. *Cost Analysis of the Columbia University Libraries for the Fiscal Year 1968–69*. Unpublished study, 1970.
Columbia University Senate Budget Review Committee. *Review of the Columbia University Budget, 1970/71*. Internal Document.
Fact-Finding Commission on Columbia Disturbances. *Crisis at Columbia*, New York: Vintage Books, 1968.
Fasana, Paul. "Determining the Cost of Library Automation." *American Library Association Bulletin*, June, 1967, pp. 97–114.
Frankel, Charles. *Education and the Barricades*. New York: Norton, 1968.
Haas, Warren J. *Administrative Organization of Columbia University Libraries*. Third Draft. Internal Document, 1970.
Kunen, James Simon. *The Strawberry Statement*. New York: Random House, 1969.
Logsdon, Richard H. "Administrative Organization of Columbia University Libraries." *College and Research Libraries*, May, 1963, pp. 219–222.
Logsdon, Richard H. "Changes in Organization at Columbia." *College and Research Libraries*, April, 1954, pp. 158–160.
Logsdon, Richard H. *Source Document on the University Libraries*. Unpublished paper, 1966.
Lucy, Mary Lou. "Columbia University Library." *Bookmark*, February, 1970, pp. 184–186.
Pei, I.M. and partners. *Planning for Columbia University*. Unpublished Study, 1970.
Shank, Russell. "Library Service to Research Laboratories of a Large University." *American Documentation*, July, 1959, pp. 221–223.
Tauber, Maurice F. "Barnard College Library: A Report on the Facilities and Services." *The College*, 1954.
Tauber, Maurice F. et al. *The Columbia University Libraries: A Report on Present and Future Needs*. New York: Columbia University Press, 1958.
Wilkinson, Billy R. "Columbia Recap: The School of Library Service During and After the Spring of 1968." *Library Journal*, July, 1969, pp. 2567–2570.

Appendix C

COLUMBIA UNIVERSITY LIBRARIES
ARL/ACE MANAGEMENT STUDY

Questionnaire Concerning
Professional Staffing Patterns

INTRODUCTION

As you are aware, a management study has been underway at Columbia for several months.
The objective of the study, using the Columbia Libraries as a case study, is to recommend
organization and staffing patterns that best meet the complex reader service and other objectives
of a university library. Critical in an analysis of this sort is a thorough understanding that
the library system is a professional enterprise consisting of individuals with varying qualifications and career interests. Organization plans need to be patterned so as to enhance the
effective utilization and development of staff resources, talents and interests towards achievement of established collective and individual objectives.

NOTE: This appendix is a questionnaire administered during the study to determine professional
staffing patterns at Columbia. The results of the questionnaire coupled with 150 interviews
with more than 75 library staff members and university officials provided the basic data
in the survey. In addition, extended discussions were held with several committees, division
heads and informal groups. Another questionnaire—The Likert Profile of Organizational
Characteristics questionnaire—was also used in a sample test basis to assist in assessing
staff attitudes concerning management patterns.

The purpose of this questionnaire is threefold: (1) to characterize the qualifications and background of professional staff at Columbia, (2) to evaluate the broad activity content of present staff positions and work assignments, and (3) to determine the range of professional career interests of professional staff. Your replies will provide a useful input to help the management study team formulate meaningful definitions of types of professional activities and career patterns that should be provided for in the organization and staffing plans of a university library.

Please study the questions carefully and answer each question completely. The results of the questionnaire will be tabulated and used so as to keep your individual response completely confidential. It would be appreciated if you would return your completed questionnaire in the enclosed addressed envelope by Wednesday, April 7, 1971.

BACKGROUND

1. Name _____   2. Age _____

3. Position Title _____   4. Library Unit _____

5. Years in Position (Work Assignment) _____   6. Years at Columbia _____

7. Years as Professional Librarian _____

8. Please list current University and Library committees of which you are presently a member and indicate any officer positions held.

9. Please describe in your own words the duties and responsibilities of your present position or work assignment.

ACADEMIC TRAINING AND QUALIFICATIONS

10. Please list all formal academic undergraduate and advanced *degree programs* you have completed or are currently engaged in.

Institution Attended	Years Attended	Major/Minor or Subject Field	Degree Received If Any and Year Conferred	Anticipated Completion Date If Still Engaged in Program

11. Please list all formal but *nondegree* academic programs you have completed or are currently engaged in.

Institution Attended	Years Attended	Subject Field

CURRENT PROFESSIONAL DEVELOPMENT ACTIVITIES

12. Please list other professional training programs, e.g., workshops, seminars, etc. you participated in during the past two years.

Title of Training Program	Training Program Provided/ Sponsored by	Subject Covered	Approximate Number Hours Spent

13. Please list current memberships in professional associations noting special committee and officer positions you have held in the past two years:

14. Please identify any speeches made, articles written, consulting projects outside Columbia, or other similar professional activities engaged in during the past two years.

PROFESSIONAL EXPERIENCE AT COLUMBIA AND ELSEWHERE

15. Please list, with most recent first, the professional positions (by position title) you have held *at institutions other than Columbia,* indicating the unit attached to and the length of time employed in the position.

Name of Organization	Position Title(s)	Name of Unit	Years in Position

16. Please list, with most recent mentioned first, the positions (work assignments) you have held *in the Columbia Library System* indicating the library unit attached to and the length of time employed in the position.

Position Title(s) or Work Assignment	Library Unit	Years in Position

17. *Please check which of the following best describes* how you obtained your first position in the Columbia Library System.

_____ I was contacted by the Columbia representatives while completing library school and subsequently invited to join the system to fill a specific position.

_____ I was contacted by Columbia representatives to apply for a position open while at another institution.

_____ I contacted Columbia on my own while at another library requesting consideration for position openings.

_____ I interviewed Columbia representatives while visiting my library school.

_____ I contacted Columbia on my own while at library school requesting consideration for position openings, since Columbia representatives did not interview at my school.

_____ I was made aware of openings at Columbia by a friend then on the library staff at Columbia, made application and was hired.

_____ I was made aware of openings at Columbia through newspaper and/or journal advertisements and submitted an application which subsequently was accepted.

Other (please elaborate). _____

_____

_____

18. If you have held more than one position at Columbia, please check which of the following *best reflects* the process by which you obtained your present position.

_____ I knew of the position opening, *made formal application,* and was subsequently made an offer.

_____ I knew of the position, but *did not make formal application,* and was subsequently made an offer.

_____ I was unaware of the opening until invited to fill the position.

Other (please elaborate). _____

_____

_____

19. Please check which of the following best describes how you currently learn about openings in the Columbia Library System that you might apply for.

_____ I depend upon my supervisors to identify openings.

_____ I depend upon informal means, e.g., word of mouth to learn of openings.

_____ I depend upon the personnel office to contact me if openings exist for which I might be considered.

_____ I depend upon my own initiative to inquire at the personnel office.

Other (please elaborate). _____

_____

_____

ACTIVITIES RELATED TO YOUR CURRENT POSITION AND TO PROFESSIONAL CAREER INTERESTS

20. Does your present position (work assignment) fulfill and satisfy your professional career interests _____Yes_____No. If *No,* have you identified to appropriate officials in the library system the type(s) of position you would be interested in filling in the future. _____Yes_____No.

21. The purpose of this question is (1) to identify distinct activities in which professional staff at Columbia are engaged; and (2) to determine the activities that most satisfy (or least satisfy) the professional career interests of individual staff.

The question should be approached in three steps:

(1) Read over thoroughly the list of 15 activities in Column A before answering the question.

(2) Please check (√) in Column B the extent to which each of the 15 activities is involved in the work you perform in your present position (work assignment).

(3) Please check (√) in Column C the extent to which each of the 15 activities reflects your long-term professional career interest.

Upon completion of the question, please be certain you have placed a check (√) next to each activity in both Column A and Column B.

Column A	Column B			Column C		
	How Much Involved in My Present Position			Extent to Which Activity Reflects My Long-Term Professional Career Interests		
	Directly Engaged In Much of My Time	Directly Engaged In Periodically	Not at All Engaged In	Best Reflects	Somewhat Reflects	Not at All Reflects
1. Instruction and orientation programs, relating library resources and services to students and faculty	___	___	___	___	___	___
2. Comprehensive reference and bibliographic services to users with research needs.	___	___	___	___	___	___
3. Selection of library materials and collection development.	___	___	___	___	___	___
4. Materials acquisition including bibliographic verification, ordering materials, maintaining records, and billing.	___	___	___	___	___	___
5. Cataloging, classifying and indexing new materials requiring original cataloging.	___	___	___	___	___	___
6. Maintenance and preservation of library collections including discarding, binding, and generally caring for the physical state of library materials.	___	___	___	___	___	___
7. Supervision of complex processing activities such as searching, filing, card preparation, cataloging with LC copy, checking shelf lists, checking in and discharging circulation materials, etc. often involving numbers of nonprofessional staff.	___	___	___	___	___	___
8. Overall management responsibility for a library unit including collection development, user services, staff utilization, and general operations.	___	___	___	___	___	___
9. Personnel matters including recruitment, compensation plans, career development programs and other areas such as long-range planning of library staff requirements.	___	___	___	___	___	___
10. Financial and budgeting matters including involvement in budgets preparation, fiscal control procedures, cost analyses, and other similar financial concerns.	___	___	___	___	___	___
11. Overall long-range planning for the library system as a whole to define priorities, objectives, relations to the university and academic departments, formulate overall policies.	___	___	___	___	___	___
12. Facilities and space management including the effective utilization of physical space, available facilities, library security, and other such matters.	___	___	___	___	___	___

	Column A		*Column B*			*Column C*	
			How Much Involved in My Present Position			Extent to Which Activity Reflects My Long-Term Professional Career Interests		
			Directly Engaged In Much of My Time	*Directly Engaged In Periodically*	*Not at All Engaged In*	*Best Reflects*	*Somewhat Reflects*	*Not at All Reflects*
13.	Operations research, systems development and computer applications.		____	____	____	____	____	____
14.	Development of library programs utilizing nonbook resources such as audio visual materials, microforms, and other media.		____	____	____	____	____	____
15.	Teaching and research in library related subject fields.		____	____	____	____	____	____

22. Please identify the number of the activity listed above that *best describes* your current position or work assignment and estimate the percent of your time you typically are engaged directly in the activity (e.g., 45%–100%).

_____ Activity Number
_____ Percent time engaged in

Index

209